DAILY

Inspiration

FOR

DIRECTION

with Devotional Prayer Points

SUNDAY DAVID EBHOMENMEN

WESTBOW
PRESS®
A DIVISION OF THOMAS NELSON
& ZONDERVAN

This book is a work of non-fiction. Unless otherwise noted, the author
and the publisher make no explicit guarantees as to the accuracy of
the information contained in this book and in some cases, names
of people and places have been altered to protect their privacy.

WestBow Press books may be ordered through booksellers or by contacting:

WestBow Press
A Division of Thomas Nelson & Zondervan
1663 Liberty Drive
Bloomington, IN 47403
www.westbowpress.com
844-714-3454

Scripture taken from the King James Version of the Bible.

ISBN: 978-1-6642-0325-9 (sc)
ISBN: 978-1-6642-0326-6 (e)

Library of Congress Control Number: 2020916236

Print information available on the last page.

WestBow Press rev. date: 09/02/2020

BIOGRAPHY

My name is Pastor, Sunday David Ebhomemen. It brings me great joy to write this book that will help many souls who are not yet saved as well as believers all over the world who needs to be refresh and rekindled with the Word of God. I began my journal years ago when I didn't know God. I was lost and not sure what direction my life was going in. As a young boy, I attended Saint Mary catholic primary school from 1981 to 1987. From 1989 to 1995 I was in secondary school, and from there I attended Ambrosia Alli University in Nigeria from 1997 to 2001 to pursue a business career. Growing into adulthood, I knew something was missing and I didn't know how to fill that void. I accepted Jesus as my Savior and received the call of God. I begin to serve as an assistant pastor before I became the General Overseer God healing and Deliverance international Gospel center where God as highly Anointed me for signs and wonders.

During the many years of serving in ministry, I have been led to give daily inspirations to help equip the Saints as well as help the unbelievers understand who God is and give them a desire to get to know Jesus as their personal Saviour. It is my desire that every man, woman, boy, girl have the opportunity to hear the gospel and received daily inspirations to help strengthen and develop them as they go throughout life on a daily basis.

One day, I met a sister in Christ who was in a dark place spiritually. I began to pour the Word of God inside of her daily. I allowed God to use me to minister by giving her daily by giving her words of inspiration. I noticed that this same woman who was in a dark place, begin to hunger and thirst for God. Instead, of me calling her to talk about the Word, she would call me and ask me about the daily inspiration. I saw God take a person who felt hopeless and gave her a thirst that no one but Him can give. This transformation encouraged me to write this book. This same lady now serves as an evangelist, partner for this book to be published and also my wife to be.

God has given me the mandate to heal the sick and bring deliverance to those who are bound. God bless you all as you get a copy of the book and go through it, I know you are going to give testimony about this book.

MORNING PRAYERS

DAILY SUCCESS AND DELIVERANCE PRAYER POINTS

PARENTS ARE ADVISED TO WAKE THERE CHILDREN UP EARLY SO AS TO ENABLE THEM START UP THEIR DAY WITH GOD.

1. Oh lord my God; I thank you for the gift of life, because without this gift I will not be alive today.

2. I thank you oh lord, for keeping me through the night and waking me up this morning in Jesus name.

3. I Confess my sins before you oh lord, that in any way that I have sinned against you, forgive me in the name of Jesus.

4. I cleanse myself of any sin in my life with the powerful Blood of Jesus Christ.

5. I thank you oh lord for my father, my mother, my brother and sisters, my aunties and uncles and my Children.

6. There shall be peace in my family this morning,

7. I cover the water I will be bathing with, and the food I will be eating today in the name of Jesus.

8. Father lord God, wherever I go to today, I shall find your favor and peace in the mighty name of Jesus.

9. Any plan of the enemies for me or for my family today, I destroy that plan with the Holy Ghost fire.

10. The vehicle I will be entering today and road I will be passing to wherever I am going today, I over with Holy Ghost fire.

CONTENTS

BE DIFFERENT

———— ∞◦∞ ————

Text: "Wherefore come out from among them, and be ye separate, saith the Lord, and touch not the unclean thing; and I will receive you" 2 Corinth 6:17

Standing in life and becoming all we are required to be will be extremely difficult if you have to blend with your environment. There is an ungodly demand on our lives today that will automatically hinder the purpose of God for our lives if we blend with it.

You cannot be a part of a problem you are meant to solve. Wherever we find ourselves in life we are meant to represent God there, we are supposed to stand out there and be someone that can point others to God. A decision to be different in a positive sense is a decision to be used of God in that sphere of influence that you find yourself.

Your value system must be different. What seems important to you must be different from the unbelieving world. If that is not the case, you'll realize that your choices and decisions will be exactly like unbelievers around you.

Your goals and pursuits in life must be different. For so many people their highest goals are just to feed themselves and dress smarter in the latest fashion in town. Your goals in life should include discovering God's purpose for your life and walking in the center of God's will for your life. Living your life this way will mark you for great things in life. *You must be different in your commitment to God.* For so many commitments to God is shallow and partial. Most commitments to God are for selfish reasons. Daniel made a commitment to God that was total and final. There was no way he could have survived without praying to God. The three Hebrew boys were ready to die for what they believed.

PRAYER:

In the name of Jesus I declare my freedom from everything that is unclean.

Oh make me a clean parson in Jesus name

LEARN MORE: Dan 1:8, Dan 6:6-10, Ephesians 4: 17 – 24, Leviticus 18:2-4, 1 Peter 4:3-4

*PRAYER REQUEST: Lord we declare that your word is growing and prevailing in every life reading Inspiration. Acts 19:20

INNER STRENGTH

Text: "That he would grant you, according to the riches of his glory, to be strengthened with might by his Spirit in the inner man." Eph 3:16

Man is a spirit; he has a soul and lives in a body. The real man is actually the spirit man within. The spirit man is also referred to as the inner man, the inward man or the hidden man of the heart (2 Corinth 4:16, 1 Pet 3:4).

The body is referred to as the outward man (2 Corinth 4:16). This is the physical body that carries us about.

When it comes to the conflicts of life what really matters is the state of the inner man. The inner man is either weak or strong. Even the physical body is sustained by the strength of the inner man.

This explains why even highly intellectual and extremely strong people have failed in the conflicts of life. This is the explanation for what happened between David and Goliath. Goliath was extremely strong physically; he had all the intellectual knowledge of fighting a physical battle.

David did not have all that but his inner man was strengthened. We are in a time and season of life that it takes more than physical and intellectual strength to win. We need inner fortitude.

Proverbs 24:10 says "If you faint in the day of adversity, thy strength is small". The strength here is referring to the state of the inner man. The Message bible says "If you fall to pieces in a crisis, there wasn't much to you in the first place". New Living Translation says "If you fail under pressure, your strength is not great."

We acquire inner strength as we spend quality time meditating in the word of God. The word of God is the meal for the inner man. We also receive inner strength as we fast and pray in the Spirit consistently.

PRAYER:

In the name of Jesus I receive inner strength from within.

A Prayer for Wisdom and Strength Daily

You are a miracle-working God. Give me a vision for what freedom looks like

for me. Give me faith to believe You for my miracle. Show me what makes me tired. Show me what masters me and slows me down. Help me to lose my taste for that which weakens me, and acquire a taste for that which strengthens me. Heal me from the inside out! Help me to make the necessary changes. I want to participate with You in my healing process. Awaken fresh life in me! In Jesus' Name, Amen.

A Prayer for Strength When You're At Your Weakest Lord Jesus, give me the strength to stick it out over the long haul—not the grim strength of gritting my teeth but the glory-strength God gives. It is strength that endures the unendurable and spills over into joy, thanking the Father who makes me strong enough to take part in everything bright and beautiful that he has for me. Jesus, give me strength in my weakness

LEARN MORE: 2 Corinth 4:16, Jude 20, Deuteronomy 33:25, Psalm 139:16, Psalm 84:5-7, Psalm 84.

PRAYER REQUEST: Lord cause the entrance of your word through Inspiration to guide, lead and direct your people daily. Ecc 10:10

JOURNEY OF FAITH

———————⬡⬡⬡———————

Text: "Now faith is the substance of things hoped for, the evidence of things not seen. For by it the elders obtained a good report." Heb 11:1-2

By the help of the Holy Spirit today I want to introduce you to something we'll be looking at in a couple of days. Please fasten your seat belt as we delve into the subject of faith afresh. I'm sure you will be inspired.

Life is a journey and it will require the operation of faith to truly travel this journey. The journey into destiny is purely a journey of faith. The only means of getting into God's great destiny for our lives is by faith. There will always be reasons in the natural, in the economy, in medical reports etc. that wants to slow us down or completely hinder the fulfillment of God's destiny for our lives. But by faith we can choose to live above the circumstances of life. There may be challenges, delays, disappointments, health issues and so on along the journey of life but none of them should be a reason for failure.

THE NATURE OF FAITH.

1. Faith is not a passive word but an active word –* We don't just wait for things to change, we engage faith to change things.

2. Faith is never hidden, it's always demonstrated –* Faith is demonstrated in the steps we take and how we respond to life.

3. Faith is not a silent force, but a speaking force –* Faith is majorly expressed by saying something. Faith requires that we speak out in agreement with God.

4. Faith is not a sitting force but a doing force, In the next couple of days we'll be looking closely at this subject from different perspectives. This is an aspect of our lives that needs constant attention. The level of your faith can never be too much. The more your faith grows the better for you.

5. And without faith it is impossible to please Him, for he who comes to God must believe that He is and that He is a rewarded of those who seek Him. *Hebrews 11:6

6. To You, O LORD, I lift up my soul. O my God, in You I trust, Do not let me be ashamed; Do not let my enemies exult over me. *Psalm 25:1-2*

7. *Proverbs 29:25 The fear of man brings a snare, But he who trusts in the LORD will be exalted.

1 Peter 1:21 who through Him are believers in God, who raised Him from the dead and gave Him glory, so that your faith and hope are in God.

*John 14:1 Do not let your heart be troubled; believe in God, believe also in Me.

John 3:16 For God so loved the world, that He gave His only begotten Son, that whoever believes in Him shall not perish, but have eternal life.

*John 6:68-69 Simon Peter answered Him, "Lord, to whom we shall go? You have words of eternal life. "We have believed and have come to know that you are the Holy One of God."

CONFESSION:

My faith is growing and triumphant.

LEARN MORE: Rom 4:17-21, 2 Thess 1:3

*PRAYER REQUEST: Lord we ask for a fresh outpouring of the Holy Spirit for fresh revelation of the word through Inspiration. Prov 1:23

STEPS OF FAITH 1

———— ∞∞∞ ————

Text: "By faith Abraham, when he was called to go out into a place which he should after receive for an inheritance obeyed; and he went out, not knowing whither he went." Heb 11:8

Taking steps into the unknown – this is a major step of faith that we'll be required to take at one time or the other in our lives. Abraham was already and old man. It would have been irrational to ask him to leave where he was. He had been in this place for so long. He had to leave the familiar for the unknown. There is always an apprehension in the heart of man when there is a need to change location, change a job or make other necessary changes around our lives.

The irony about life is that what has become known to us today was once an unknown. It therefore means that whatever looks like the unknown today will soon become the known. Abraham left the familiar for the unknown. If he had remained where he had always been the blessings of the covenant would have eluded him. If you remain where you are, where you have always been, doing all you have always done your life may not go beyond what it is now.

We must recognize when something is no longer working in our lives and God is prompting us towards a change. The greatest blessings in our lives are reserved in the unknown places. If you embrace what looks like unknown today after a while it will become the known and we may get attached to it again. As you embrace the unknown at God's promptings there will be fresh opportunities in your life to experience something new that God wants to do in your life.

Abraham did not even question God because he knew that God knows what is best. He was so yielded to God. Faith is actually yielding ourselves to God's counsel for our lives even when it does not make sense. Trust God with your life.

PRAYER:

Lord I yield myself to you afresh today. Work in me and for me your good plans.

Thank you for helping us to make it through this difficult year. Thank you that you've carried us through the uncertainty of deep waters, through the flames of trials, and through the pain of hard losses. We are constantly aware of how much we need you, your grace your strength, your power working through even the toughest days.

Help us to keep our focus first on you this season. Please forgive us for giving too much time and attention to other things, for looking to other people before coming to you first. Help us to reflect again, on you. Thank you that you came to give new life, peace, hope, and joy. Thank you that your power is made perfect in our weakness.

LEARN MORE: Ps 125:1

PRAYER REQUEST: Lord orders the steps of everyone reading Inspiration into your plans and purpose daily. Psalm 37:23

*PRAYING FOR PRISONERS:

Lord we ask for unusual grace to be poured afresh upon every prison minister to effectively carry out their assignment with supernatural accomplishments. John 1:16

STEPS OF FAITH 2

Text: "By faith he forsook Egypt, not fearing the wrath of the King: for he endured, as seeing him who is invisible." Heb 11:27, Faith sees the invisible and expects the impossible – Faith has a unique way of seeing. Faith sees beyond what is physically revealed to the human eye. This is why the faith life is completely strange to so many people. If we are going to walk with God we have to see beyond the obvious. We must clearly in our spirit what God is saying even when physical eye cannot see them. Faith sees the unusual.

The servant of Elisha saw with his physical eyes the armies of the Syrians while Elisha was seeing the chariots of fire that was protecting them. God had to open the inner eyes of the young servant to see beyond what the physical eye was seeing. Faith is seeing with the inner eyes what the physical eyes cannot see. In this case we are not just seeing with our physical eyes but with the heart.

Faith expects what others say is impossible. Having an expectation generated and rooted in the word of God is a major part of walking by faith. We must see, declare and celebrate God's possibilities in every situation of life. Expectation is magnetic; it draws the object of our expectation into our lives. What you don't expect you don't have the right to experience.

If all you are seeing is what everybody around you is seeing then you will be limited to what goes on in that environment. We must see beyond the immediate and the obvious. It was possible for Moses to run away from Egypt because he saw the invisible. He knew that God had a greater plan for him. The scripture says "While we look not at the things which are seen, but at the things which are not seen: for the things which are seen are temporal;but the things which are not seen are eternal." 2 Corinth 4:18.

THANKSGIVING:

Thank you Lord for the great plans you have for our lives. Thank you because your counsels are bigger than the immediate challenges around us.

THANKSGIVING FOR PRAYER POINT

1. Father In The Name Of Jesus, I proclaim that there is no one like You even among the gods. You are Glorious In Holiness and Fearful In Praises. OH God. Accept my praises in Jesus name.

2. My Father, I will sing your praises aloud in the presence of kings and leaders of this world in Jesus name.

3. Father, I thank you for your divine help that I have enjoyed in my life. If I begin to mention them I will run out of numbers. Thank you Father in Jesus Name.

4. I confess today that the LORD lives! Blessed be the Lord, Let the name of the Lord be exalted, The Rock of my salvation! in Jesus name.

5. Father in the name of Jesus, i declare that you reign above the heavens and the earth, none can compare to your greatness.

6. My Father and My God I will give praises to your name as long as I live And have the breath in my nostrils in Jesus name.

7. Jehovah, I will praise you because you are a glorious God, and a merciful Father.

8. Father, I give praises to your name because you are the God that silences all my enemies in Jesus name.

9. Oh Lord, I praise your name for the wonders of your creations that you created for the benefit of mankind in Jesus name.

10. Oh Lord, I thank you for creating me in your image and likeness in Jesus name.

LEARN MORE: Prov 23:18, Heb 11:1-6

PRAYER REQUEST: Lord we declare that the quickening power of your Spirit will be at work as the you read Inspiration daily. John 6:63

Inspiring Men! *"The life of a believer is ultimately defined in terms of eternity. Whatever is not of eternal value is eternally useless. How much of your pursuit is of eternal worth. That's the ultimate worth of your life and not the cars and the muscles" BE A MAN!*

STEPS OF FAITH 3

Text: "Run now, I pray thee, to meet her, and say unto her, is it well with thee? Is it well with thy husband? Is it well with thy child? And she answered, it is well." 2 King 4:26

Agreeing with God in every situation irrespective of what is happening around you - This woman in our anchor scripture lost her only son. It must have been a devastating experience for her. The natural thing would have been for her to be crying and confused. The prophet sent a message to her to find out what was wrong and she stated categorically "it's well". Why will she say that when it's obvious that her child was dead. She simply took side with God. She was not denying what happened, she was simply agreeing with God rather than the situation. When things have gone wrong around you it's never an indication that things have gone wrong with God. God's position never changes. If you agree with your situation you have given the enemy an edge over you. One thing that reveal that you are agreeing with your situation is when the problem dictates what you say and how you respond. It's obvious that the death of the child did not dictate this woman's response. She responded in faith not minding what people will say. The scriptures speaks about Abraham that "And being not weak in faith, he considered not his own body now dead, when he was about an hundred years old, neither yet the deadness of Sarah's womb." Rom 4:19. He did not agree with his situation but rather with what God has said. God has said you are the head and not the tail; agree with God even though you are at the lowest ebb in life. The word says we are blessed with all spiritual blessings, so we can go ahead and declare that we are blessed even though we don't have a bank account to our name. Please agree with God today.

PRAYER:

Lord I agree with your word as the final say over every issue of my life.Whatever you have said is the final authority on my life.

LEARN MORE: Amos 3:3, Lk 1:38

PRAYER REQUEST: Lord cause your people to behold wondrous things out of your word daily. Psalm 119:18

Inspiring Men!

I have been challenged on few occasions on why I'm addressing only men. I agree that women have their own issues. But as men God has placed us as the head. We must behave as one. We can rise above what a woman does right or not and choose to be a model .

PRAYING FOR PRISONERS:

Please join me daily!

Lord we ask for a fresh outpouring of the Holy Spirit in every prison house bringing men and women to conviction of salvation and direction in life. Joel 2:28-29

1. Father, i thank you for the grace to be alive and to sing your praises to you today in Jesus name.

2. Dear Lord, cause me to have new testimonies that I may offer more thanksgiving to your name in the midst of the saints in Jesus name.

3. Dear Lord, I lift your name higher, above all other names, above everything in heaven and in earth in Jesus name.

4. Oh Lord, I will boast of your goodness, and your great kindness all day long and I praise you for being my God in Jesus name.

5. Oh Lord, I praise you for fighting the battles of my life in Jesus name

6. Oh Lord, I will praise You, in the midst of my trials, you are indeed the reason why I am happy

7. Oh Lord, I magnify your name and I acknowledge your greatness in Jesus name.

8. Oh Lord, I join the congregation of brethren to give praises to you for you have done great things in my life in Jesus name.

9. Oh Lord, I praise your name today because only the living can praise your name, the dead cannot praise you

10. Oh Lord, I praise you today for you are good and your mercies endures forever in Jesus name

PAGE 7.

STEPS OF FAITH 4

Text: "By faith Moses, when he was come to years, refused to be called the son of Pharaoh's daughter" Heb 11:24

Embracing God's plan and purpose for our lives even when no one believes in it – In the days of Moses we don't really have any account if there were any other son that was born to Pharaoh. The only emphasis was to the daughter of Pharaoh. There was every possibility that Moses would have become the next Pharaoh in Egypt. In those days the Pharaoh was like the American president. Apart from this he had so much privilege that he enjoyed in the palace. Refusing to be called Pharaoh's daughter means he was going to lose all the privileges. Everybody must have felt that he was crazy. To make the matter worse he forsook Egypt completely. Moses knew very clearly that God had a better and a greater plan for his life. He began to sense within himself that he was supposed to be a deliverer and not a Pharaoh. He made an initial wrong attempt to do this while he was still in Egypt. Divine agenda is far better than earthly placements. God's agenda for your life is far better and greater than any human placement.

If you are going to experience all that God has in store for you there must be a resolve in you to embrace God's plan for you even when no one believes in it. The irony about life is that people around you will hardly believe in what you set out to do initially. All that matters is that God believes in us and we believe in ourselves. A wise man said "You may succeed if no one believes in you, but you will never succeed if you don't believe in yourself." Don't wait for the whole world to endorse what you are passionate about; you may have to wait forever. When I started writing this devotional and publishing it some people had their reservations but thank God I kept at it. It's been about seven years in print now.

DECLARATION:

I believe in God's plans for me. I will embrace it with all my heart and strength. I will rather sink with God than shine without G

ETERNAL SOURCE

Text: "Ye are of God, little children, and have overcome them: because greater is he that is in you, than he that is in the world."1 John 4:4

Everything God created was designed to depend on its source for sustenance. This is why staying in water is not an option for a fish, but a must. If you have ever seen a fish outside water you will understand how helpless the fish is without water. Every plant came out of soil, if you take it out of soil it withers away gradually. All these establish the truth that everything created depends on its source for life.

From our anchor scripture today "Ye are of God" from the Greek translation means "You originate from God". We did not merely originate from our parents but essentially we originated from God. It therefore means that God is our eternal source. Everything we'll ever need in life is found in God.

For the fish to keep receiving support from the water it has to stay in water. For plant to keep drawing nourishment from the soil it has to remain attached to the soil. In the same light to keep drawing from God we must stay attached to God.

Staying attached to God is more than just going to church. It practically means developing an intimate relationship with God, it's possible to go to church all your life and not have an intimate relationship with

God. This is a relationship that comes from the understanding that there is nothing you can do without God. Knowing God and getting close to him becomes the heartbeat of your life. As important as your degree is, it has no capacity to become your source. Your job is a channel but never your source. No human being is rich enough to be your source. Ultimately God is your eternal source. All you need in life is available in Him.

PRAYER:

Lord by your Spirit help me to know you. Help me to stay connected to you as my eternal source.

*LEARN MORE: John 15:4-6

John 17:3
And this is eternal life, that they know you the only true God, and Jesus Christ whom you have sent.

2 Peter 3:9
The Lord is not slow to fulfill his promise as some count slowness, but is patient toward you, not wishing that any should perish, but that all should reach repentance.

Hebrews 4:15
For we do not have a high priest who is unable to sympathize with our weaknesses, but one who in every respect has been tempted as we are, yet without sin.

1 Timothy 2:5
For there is one God, and there is one mediator between God and men, the man Christ Jesus,

Hebrews 11:3
By faith we understand that the universe was created by the word of God, so that what is seen was not made out of things that are visible.

Romans 8:29
For those whom he foreknew he also predestined to be conformed to the image of his Son, in order that he might be the firstborn among many brothers.

John 17:5
Nehemiah 9:5

Then the Levites, Jeshua, Kadmiel, Bani, Hashabneiah, Sherebiah, Hodiah, Shebaniah and Pethahiah, said, "Arise, bless the LORD your God forever and ever! O may Your glorious name be blessed And exalted above all blessing and praise!

Deuteronomy 32:40
'Indeed, I lift up My hand to heaven, And say, as I live forever,

Deuteronomy 33:27
"The eternal God is a dwelling place, And underneath are the everlasting arms; And He drove out the enemy from before you, And said, 'Destroy!'

Job 36:26
"Behold, God is exalted, and we do not know Him; The number of His years is unsearchable.

Psalm 48:14
For such is God, Our God forever and ever; He will guide us until death.

And now, Father, glorify me in your own presence with the glory that I had with you before the world existed.

PRAYER REQUEST: Lord order the steps of everyone reading Inspiration today into divine purpose and plans Psalm 37:23.

*"It's common to see young people with grey hair but doing many foolish things. Grey hair is never a sign of wisdom. Age does not equal maturity. Wisdom is a function of being guided by God's word in thoughts and deeds.

WINNING STRATEGIES 1

———— ⌘ ————

Text: "For everyone born of God overcomes the world. This is the victory that overcomes the world, even our faith." 1 John 5:4 NIV

The strategies of our warfare are not man made strategies but based on God that is capable of winning any battle of life. If you are going to stand out in life you must understand that you cannot afford to handle life the same way unbelievers will handle it. We have strategies in God that far exceed what exist in this world. The weapons of Saul were good but inadequate to handle Goliath until someone with a higher weapon came on the scene.

The strategies start from an understanding that we are born of God. We are direct product of God .We originates from him and whatever comes out of God carries everything that God is. Have you not read that we are partakers of the divine nature?

By mere birth we are designed and fashioned to overcome whatever comes our way. There is really no category of the challenge of life that is bigger than what we can handle. With this understanding we don't have to run from any challenge but run towards it. That was exactly what David did to Goliath.1 Sam 17:48.

Winning strategies for you as a believer also includes seeing yourself as bigger than this world. The God of the universe is your father. He said to me recently "I am committed to your life more than you can ever imagine". God is for you, God is with you and God is in you. That is a three -fold cord of partnership with God that cannot be broken. No force of hell can beat that.

When it seems all hope is gone hold on to these spiritual realities, it's your strategy for winning.

Let's see what it did for Jehoshaphat...

Then the Spirit of the Lord came on Jahaziel...as he stood in the assembly. He said: "Listen, King Jehoshaphat and all who live in Judah and Jerusalem! This is what the Lord says to you: 'Do not be afraid or discouraged because of this vast army. For the battle is not yours, but God's." 2 Chron. 20:14-15

The Spirit showed up. God gave instructions on how to win and he also gave his presence that said, "I will be with you."

When we seek God, we find him.
When we find his face, he faces us with real truth.
When we know where our help comes from, our help often comes.

Warfare, Strategies In

Joshua 8:5
"Then I and all the people who are with me will approach the city. And when they come out to meet us as at the first, we will flee before them.

Judges 7:16
He divided the 300 men into three companies, and he put trumpets and empty pitchers into the hands of all of them, with torches inside the pitchers.

Judges 20:32
The sons of Benjamin said, "They are struck down before us, as at the first." But the sons of Israel said, "Let us flee that we may draw them away from the city to the highways."

Genesis 14:14
When Abram heard that his relative had been taken captive, he led out his trained men, born in his house, three hundred and eighteen, and went in pursuit as far as Dan.

Genesis 32:7
Then Jacob was greatly afraid and distressed; and he divided the people who were with him, and the flocks and the herds and the camels, into two companies;

Joshua 8:3-25
So Joshua rose with all the people of war to go up to Ai; and Joshua chose 30,000 men, valiant warriors, and sent them out at night. He commanded them, saying, "See, you are going to ambush the city from behind it. Do not go very far from the city, but all of you be ready. "Then I and all the people who are with me will approach the city. And when they come out to meet us as at the first, we will flee before them. They will come out after us until we have drawn them away from the city, for they will say, 'They are fleeing before us as at the first.' So we will flee before them. "And you shall rise from your ambush and take possession of the city, for the LORD your God will deliver it into your hand. "Then it will be when you have seized the city, that you shall set the city on fire. You shall do it according to the word of the LORD. See, I have commanded you." So Joshua sent them away, and they went to the place of ambush and remained between Bethel and Ai, on the west side of Ai; but Joshua spent that night among the people. Now Joshua rose early in the morning and mustered the people, and he went up with the elders of Israel before the people to Ai. Then all the people of war who were with him went up and drew near and arrived in front of the city, and camped on the

north side of Ai. Now there was a valley between him and Ai. And he took about 5,000 men and set them in ambush between Bethel and Ai, on the west side of the city. So they stationed the people, all the army that was on the north side of the city, and its rear guard on the west side of the city, and Joshua spent that night in the midst of the valley. It came about when the king of AI saw it, that the men of the city hurried and rose up early and went out to meet Israel in battle, he and all his people at the appointed place before the desert plain. But he did not know that there was an ambush against him behind the city. Joshua and all Israel pretended to be beaten before them, and fled by the way of the wilderness. And all the people who were in the city were called together to pursue them, and they pursued Joshua and were drawn away from the city. So not a man was left in Ai or Bethel who had not gone out after Israel, and they left the city unguarded and pursued Israel. Then the LORD said to Joshua, "Stretch out the javelin that is in your hand toward Ai, for I will give it into your hand." So Joshua stretched out the javelin that was in his hand toward the city. The men in ambush rose quickly from their place, and when he had stretched out his hand, they ran and entered the city and captured it, and they quickly set the city on fire. When the men of Ai turned back and looked, behold, the smoke of the city ascended to the sky, and they had no place to flee this way or that, for the people who had been fleeing to the wilderness turned against the pursuers. When Joshua and all Israel saw that the men in ambush had captured the city and that the smoke of the city ascended, they turned back and slew the men of AI. The others came out from the city to encounter them, so that they were trapped in the midst of Israel, some on this side and some on that side; and they slew them until no one was left of those who survived or escaped. But they took alive the king of Ai and brought him to Joshua. Now when Israel had finished killing all the inhabitants of Ai in the field in the wilderness where they pursued them, and all of them were fallen by the edge of the sword until they were destroyed, then all Israel returned to Ai and struck it with the edge of the sword. All who fell that day, both men and women, were 12,000--all the people of Ai

Judges 7:16-23

He divided the 300 men into three companies, and he put trumpets and empty pitchers into the hands of all of them, with torches inside the pitchers. He said to them, "Look at me and do likewise. And behold, when I come to the outskirts of the camp, do as I do. "When I and all who are with me blow the trumpet, then you also blow the trumpets all around the camp and say, 'For the LORD and for Gideon.

So Gideon and the hundred men who were with him came to the outskirts of the camp at the beginning of the middle watch, when they had just posted the watch; and they blew the trumpets and smashed the pitchers that were in their hands. When the three companies blew the trumpets and broke the pitchers, they held the torches in their left hands and the trumpets in their right hands for blowing, and cried, "A sword for the LORD and for Gideon!" Each stood in his place around the camp; and all the army ran, crying out as they fled. When they blew 300 trumpets, the LORD set the sword of one against another even throughout the whole army; and the army fled as far as Beth-shittah toward Zererah, as far as the edge of Abel-meholah, by Tabbath. The men of Israel were summoned from Naphtali and Asher and all Manasseh, and they pursued Midian.

WINNING STRATEGIES 2

—————∞∞∞—————

Text: "Though a host should encamp against me,my heart shall not fear: Though war should rise against me, in this will I be confident." Psalm 27:3

David is a typical example of a man who was not spared at all, he had his own share of all manner of challenges but he came out victorious in each of them.

What we go through is not as important as how we go through them. Our attitude is what determines the outcome of the challenges that confronts us.

No matter what happens retain your confidence. This was clearly seen in the life of David. David said "No matter what happens I will be confident" (Paraphrased).

Confidence on three (3) levels:

* Confidences in God -* Don't ever lose sight of that. God remains what he is. The circumstances of life does not change him. He's forever faithful.

* Confidence in yourself –* The ability of God in you is an indication that you are no longer a victim to the circumstances of life. The victory of Christ on the cross is credited to your account.

* Confidence about life –* Understand that life will get better for you. Understand that all things are working together for your good. As long as God has not given up on you refuse to give up on life. The profit of the earth is for all and you must have your own portion.

These are strategies in the realm of the Spirit that guarantees your winning.

CONFESSION:

God is on my side. I will see the goodness of the Lord in the land of the living. The victory of Christ has become my victory. His ability has become my ability.

LEARN MORE: Ps 27:13-14

*PRAYER REQUEST:Lord grant unto your people afresh the Spirit of wisdom and revelation in the knowledge of you. Eph 1:17-18.

WINNING STRATEGIES 3

Text: "I have set the Lord always before me: Because he is at my right hand I shall not be moved." Ps 16:8

The scripture above is a major strategy in winning the conflicts of life. This simply means to see God in every situation of life. Don't see him as the one responsible but rather as your way out. See God as the solution.

Don't set your eyes on the problem. Whatever takes your attention and focus naturally magnifies itself in your life. When we focus on God we make him bigger than the situation.

As David was facing Goliath he was seeing beyond the Giant, his eyes was on the great God. If you check the story carefully his emphasis was God. Saul and the other people were talking of how big Goliath was while David spoke of how big God was. He said "...The Lord that delivered me out of the paw of the lion ...he will deliver me out of the hand of this philistine..." He said "...This day will the Lord deliver thee into my hand...".1 Sam 17:37, 46

David had an unshakable awareness of God's presence. His boldness was based on that.

This strategy is found all over scripture. Job had a terrible affliction on his life but his words were "And though after my skin worms destroy this body, yet in my flesh shall I see God". Job 19:26

The body of Abraham and his wife were dead according to scripture. Their bodies were useless re productively but Abraham did not "consider" that, he did not focus on it. His focus was on God that quickens the dead.

When we see God in every situation it helps us to keep our hope alive and to maintain a faith response to whatever is happening. Once we focus on the problem we'll begin to stagger at the promises of God.

CONFESSION:

I see God in every challenge of life. I see God making a way for me.. I see God fighting my battles.

LEARN MORE: Job 19:25-26, Rom 4:17-21

*PRAYER REQUEST: Lord cause your word through Inspiration to daily build, inspire and direct as the people read. Acts 20:32.

YOU HAVE TO SAY IT

<small>∞∞∞</small>

Text: "For verily I say unto you, That whosoever shall say unto this mountain, Be thou removed, and be thou cast into the sea; and shall not doubt in his heart, but shall believe that those things which he saith shall come to pass; he shall have whatsoever he saith." Mk 11:23

The Word of God is full with teachings on the importance of using your tongue to chart your course and shape your future, for what you say is what you get (Mark 11:23). Every man is the character of his words; life will produce for you a harvest of what you say—good or bad. Therefore, it's very important that you always make faith declarations about your life. Someone might ask, "What if I haven't been saying anything?" Well, the trouble is, you'll still have a harvest; but it will be the wrong one. Imagine you have a garden, and you refuse to sow any seeds in it; something will definitely grow of its own accord, and that'll be weeds. Sadly, the lives of some are that way. They don't realize they have something to do about their lives, so they've assumed that "whatever will be, will be"; that's a wrong perception of life. It's not God's responsibility per se to ensure that you live in victory, dominion and prosperity. He already did all that's necessary for you to enjoy a transcendent life in Christ through the power of the Holy Spirit. It's your responsibility now to do something with what He's already given to you.

2 Peter 1:3 says, "According as his divine power hath given unto us all things that pertain unto life and godliness, through the knowledge of him that hath called us to glory and virtue." This ought to give you a new mind-set and form the basis for your faith filled confessions. You must say that you have a great life, if you're going to live it! You must acknowledge and confess that you've been called to a life of glory and virtue; that means a life of power, dominion, and excellence. The principle is, "If you don't say it, you can't have it." Remember, your life is like a garden; sow the right seeds in it by speaking the right words—words of faith—and your life will blossom.

PRAYER:

My mouth is empowered afresh today to speak words of truth and words of power. I overcome timidity of the spirit.

LEARN MORE: Jos 1:8, Prov 18:21

*PRAYER REQUEST: Thank you Lord for a new month. We take authority over the month of March. We decree that only God's counsels will stand this month. Isa 46:10.

RULES FOR
YOUR WORDS

———— ⊗⊗⊗ ————

Text: "But the men that went up with him said, we be not able to go up against the people: for they are stronger than we" Num 13:31

If you study carefully the story of the ten spies that gave evil report of what they saw in the Promised Land you'll discover that at the end of the day it was their words that became their trap. The words they spoke worked against them. What God did was simply to confirm what they said.

Today we'll look at a couple of rules that should guide our words, so that our words can always work for us.

1. Don't speak according to your size; speak according to the size of your God.

2. Don't speak how big the problems are; speak about how big the promises of God are.

3. Don't speak about what the enemy is doing; speak about what God is doing.

4. Don't speak about where you are; speak about where you are going.

5. Don't speak about what you are experiencing; speak about what you are expecting.

6. Don't speak about what you are seeing; speak about what God is saying.

7. Don't talk about the enemy; talk about God.

These major differences are clearly seeing in what the ten spies said and what Caleb and his colleague said. If we allow these rules to guide our words we'll find ourselves always speaking words of faith, words of power and words of possibilities. Just imagine if God confirms every word you have ever spoken what your life will look like. If you realist it or not that is exactly what is happening in your life right now.

God is making a way for you where there seems to be no way. All things are working together for your good. God is saying I will do a new thing in your life. God is saying I will never leave you nor forsake you. God is saying my grace is sufficient for you. His word says by the stripes of Jesus you are healed. These are words that should occupy your mouth.

CONFESSION:

All things are working for my good. The lines are fallen unto me in pleasant places, I have a goodly heritage.

LEARN MORE: Num 14:28-29

Because Abraham gave ear to my voice and kept my words, my rules, my orders, and my laws.

Exo 15:26
And he said, "If you carefully listen to the voice of Yahweh your God and you do [what is] right in his eyes and give heed to his commands and you keep all his rules, [then] I will not bring about on you any of the diseases that I brought about on Egypt, because I [am] Yahweh your healer.

Exo 18:20
And you warn them [of] the rules and the instructions, and you make known to them the way in which they must walk and the work that they must do.

Exo 34:28
And for forty days and forty nights Moses was there with the Lord, and in that time he had no food or drink. And he put in writing on the stones the words of the agreement, the ten rules of the law.

Lev 10:11
and to teach the {Israelite} all the rules that Yahweh has spoken to them {through} Moses."

Lev 18:3
You may not do those things which were done in the land of Egypt where you were living; and you may not do those things which are done in the land of Canaan where I am taking you, or be guided in your behavior by their rules.

Lev 18:4
But you are to be guided by my decisions and keep my rules, and be guided by them: I am the Lord your God.

PRAYER REQUEST: Lord we ask ask that your power will daily be available as the people read Inspiration daily to effect permanent changes in their lives. Luke 5:17

PRAYING FOR PRISONERS:

Please join me daily!

*Lord we declare every veil covering the hearts of men and women in prison from salvation be lifted. Satanic blindfolding are removed (2 Cor 4:4)

THE POTTER'S JOB

———— ∞∞ ————

Text: "O house of Israel, cannot I do with you as the potter? Saith the Lord. Behold, as the clay is in the potter's hand, so are ye in mine hand, O house of Israel." Jer 18:6

This scripture describes the kind of relationship that God seeks to have with us. The unfortunate thing is that most of the time we don't allow this relationship to work. We seem to think we know so much to handle life on our own.

The job of the potter becomes easy and possible when the clay submits to the potter. The more the clay resists the potter the more difficult it become for the potter to accomplish his task.

Usually the potter sees in the clay what the clay cannot see in itself. There is so much beauty and possibility locked up within us that God wants to reveal to the world to see. But we must understand that just as a potter works on the clay before the beauty comes out so also God seeks to work in us and on us every day. The unhindered access that God has into our lives is what brings out the beauty in our lives.

If there are areas of our lives that God has not been allowed to touch it becomes a place where the purpose of God for our lives will be hindered. If God does not have control over your relationships and the association you keep it has limited how far God can go with you.

There are those that God can never have a say in their finances. How they spend it and what they use it for is purely their decision. This will also limit what God can accomplish through them.

The potter needs an unconditional and an unhindered access to the clay, so also God wants in our lives. There should never be an area of life that God cannot correct you about.

PRAYER:

Lord my life is open and available for you. Work in me your good pleasure and do with me whatever you will.

LEARN MORE: Phil 2:13

PRAYER REQUEST: Lord fill your people afresh with the knowledge of your will in all wisdom and spiritual understanding.

PRAYING FOR PRISONERS:

Please join me daily!

*Lord for everyone who has received Christ in prison we declare that are filled with the knowledge of your will (Col 1:9

THE POTTER'S JOB 2

———— ∞∞∞ ————

Text: "And the vessel that he made of clay was marred in the hand of the potter: so he made it again another vessel, as seemed good to the potter to make it." Jer 18:4

The ultimate job of the potter is to bring out the best out of the clay. It does not matter how "marred" the clay is the potter know exactly what to do to bring out the best in the clay. We must also understand that no matter how messed up our lives are the all wise God knows exactly what to do to bring out the best in our lives.

Wherever you are and whatever you have been through God can bring out the best out of it. The circumstances of Joseph were so "marred", but God eventually brought out the best out of it. Naomi was so hopeless that she was ready to send away her two daughter in-laws, but the master potter brought the beauty out of the messed up situation. Apostle Paul was once the worst sinner. But because after the encounter with the potter he gave God an unhindered access to his life and he became the greatest Apostle that ever lived. Am so sure something great and beautiful is coming forth out of your life.

One major factor in the potter carrying out his job is for us to understand that whatever the potter wants to do is not based on what the clay wants but what "...seemed good to the potter...", we don't dictate to God. We simply allow him to do with us whatever he wills. Like the architect, God has the master plan of our lives and he knows what is best for us. The things that seemed good to us might be a direct opposite of what God had in mind. The key is to keep submitting to God on all issues. We must get to the point where we don't struggle with him any more on any issue.

CONFESSION:

The master potter is having unhindered access in my life. Working in me what seems good to him. The beauty in my life is coming forth.

MINISTERING GRACE 2

Text: "Let no corrupt communication proceed out of your mouth, but that which is good to the use of edifying, that it may minister grace to the hearers." Ephesians 4:29

We are all ministers in our sphere of influence. Once you have one or two persons that you speak to every day, you already have the privilege to minister to them. It could be your children. It could be your classmates. We have people hearing us daily.

The words of your mouth must be good. How do we define what is good or not. Simple, it must be scripturally-inclined. It must be able to pass the litmus test of the word of God. This is the best way to make the word of your mouth powerful and useful in edifying other people.

Norman Vincent Peale said some years ago that *"Christians ought to be in the business of building people up, because there are so many people today already in the demolition business".* We build up lives or demolish them by our words.

No matter what you do and where you are found God is counting on you there to encourage and build lives there. You are the minister in that place ministering grace to your hearers.

We live in a world that is full of negative news every day. Discouragement in the air. The hearts of men are failing daily for fear of the unknown. We have a unique advantage today to reach out to people in our environment. If you allow the word of God to get hold of your heart and mouth a powerful ministry can begin from your life where you are located. You don't need a pulpit to start a ministry; all you need is your mouth that is trained to minister grace to everyone that comes your way.

"Watch the way you talk. Let nothing foul or dirty come out of your mouth. Say only what helps, each word a gift." Eph 4:29 Message Bible.

PRAYER:

Lord my mouth is available to minister grace to my hearers. Build someone up through me today.

LEARN MORE: 2 Corinth 3:6, Ephesians 4:31

PRAYER REQUEST: Lord we declare that grace is continually poured forth through every word in Inspiration. John 1:16

GUIDED WITH DISCRETION

⧴⧵⧴

Text: "A good man sheathe favor, and lendeth; he will guide his affairs with discretion." Psalm 112:5

When a man or woman lacks discretion they will make a mess of God's investment in their lives. Opportunities and privileges are drawn into the mud when a man lacks discretion. The relevance of discretion is that you don't rush to take a step or say something.

Discretion is the quality of been circumspect. Circumspect refers to the ability to spot and recognize details before jumping to a conclusion. Discretion is been able to see beyond what is obvious. Similar words to circumspect include cautious, prudent and thoughtful. Discretion helps us to place the right value on situations before drawing conclusions on them. Discretion is also the ability to make wise choices and decisions. This is the ingredient that life is made of. Decisions determine direction and direction determine destination or destiny. What you put into a pot of soup determines the taste it gives you. Your life can never get better than the quality of choices and decisions that we make on a daily basis. The prodigal son made two decisions that produced two end results in his life.

1. He took a decision to live home – He took his inheritance and wasted it on riotous living. This produced poverty for him. He lost all the glory around his life.

2. He buried his shame and made a decision to go back home – With this decision his life was restored and the glory of God came back on his life.

These were two decisions with two end results made by the same person. Allow your affairs to be guided with discretion this year. Don't just do things that look right or feel right. Do things that will take you in the direction of God's plans for your life.

PRAYER:

Lord fill my heart with fresh wisdom to take the right steps this year and to go in the right direction.

LEARN MORE: Ps 32:8; 37:23

PRAYER REQUEST: Lord cause your word to run swiftly across the nations of the earth through Inspiration.

Inspiring men!

*Sir, God asked me to remind you today that there is a leadership seed in your spirit. You were designed to be a role model. The God on your inside is bigger than all that life will ever throw at you. Shine forth and let your seeds be proud of you.

STRENGTH FOR THE JOURNEY

———∞∞∞———

Text: "If thou faint in the day of adversity, thy strength is small." Prov 24:10

We stated clearly in the past that life is a journey and not necessarily a destination. The journey of 2019 ended and here we are already on the journey of 2020. We are not just talking of a physical journey that requires physical strength to handle it. We are talking of an invisible journey that requires inner strength to go through.

The journey of life place demands on our lives that may be life threatening. We need inner strength to handle them and forge ahead in life.

"...Your strength is small" In our anchor scripture talks about failure to handle the challenges that comes our way. Breaking down under the weight of the challenges of life. Everyone goes through one form of challenge or another. The ability to stand up to them is what matters. It's not really the enormity of the challenges that defeats us but the smallness of our inner strength. The stronger we become the more equipped we are to face whatever comes our way.

The inner strength is built in proportion to the word of God made available to the inner man. The more we starve our spirit man of the word of God the weaker it becomes in handling life. When we are weak within we'll find ourselves getting easily discouraged. This may also result in physical weakness. A Yoruba adage says *"It takes inner strength to sustain the outer strength."*

We take on strength for the journey of life as we become conscious of who we are and what we carry. We are joint heirs with Christ. We are so connected to him in an inseparable union. He is the vine we are the branches. It therefore means that we are not handling anything on our own. We must also understand that the greater one dwells within us. We are never alone. A sense of being alone produces weakness in a man.

PRAYER:

I decree strength in my inner man to face every challenge this year and to go over the walls.

LEARN MORE: Ps 18:29-32, Eph 3:16

PRAYER REQUEST: Lord we decree that this week will be a moment of divers encounters with your word through Inspiration. 2 Cor 3:18

Inspiring men!

*The position of a man is a privilege. We did not apply for it. It was a divine decision. We must be able to humble ourselves before God and allow his wisdom to flow through us for the benefit of those he has placed in our trust

CALLED OF GOD

—∞∞∞—

Text: "Who hath saved us, and called us with an holy calling, not according to our works, but according to his own purpose and grace, which was given us in Christ Jesus before the world began." 2 Tim 1:9.

What an awesome scripture we have here. Every word here is loaded. We'll just attempt today to look at a few issues here.

God has saved us. Not because we requested for it, it was purely a divine decision. The whole arrangement of redemption was God's decision even before the world began. We are saved not by our efforts, there was nothing in the natural we could have done to merit salvation. Salvation was based on divine purpose and grace given to us in Christ Jesus. Thank God we are saved; in spite of how sinful we were He saved us according to his purpose and grace.

Salvation is actually the first expression of the purpose of God for man. When a man receives the message of the gospel and they are saved they automatically enter into a sphere of life in which the purpose of God can come to pass in their lives. What an awesome privilege we have. Each one of us as believers has the greatest privilege of all humanity to fulfill the purpose of God for our lives. We'll explore this in a deeper way.

Did you notice again in our anchor scripture that we are called of God? This is actually our central focus for today. Being called of God is not reserved only for the Apostles, Prophets and Bishops. Each one of us as believers has a holy calling on our lives. You are a special breed. God placed something unique and awesome in your life. Your life should never end up ordinary like someone who is not saved. We are called of God to make a difference in this world and to leave footprints in the sand of life. My prayer for you is that this year will be a unique year for you in every way.

CONFESSION :

I have a holy calling on my life. I was called and equipped to make a difference in this world.

LEARN MORE: 1 Pet 2:9

PRAYER REQUEST: Lord order the steps of your people afresh to walk in the center of your purpose for their lives. Psalm 37:23

PRAYING FOR PRISONERS:

Please join me daily!

Lord we ask for supernatural intervention in prison houses across this nation (Mention your nation) to become places where lives are changed and molded to fulfill destiny.

The Lord reward you!

Inspiring men!

*One of the greatest victory in the life of a man is when he becomes humble, teachable and correctable. So many issues will be resolved in a man's life when this happens. There is no limit to how far God can take such a man.

ESTABLISHED IN TRUTH

Text: "Wherefore I will not be negligent to put you always in remembrance of these things, though ye know them, and be established in the present truth." 2 Pet 1:12

The Devil operates and thrives in an arena where darkness dominates. Darkness here is an expression of ignorance. The devil does not mind seeing you come to church as long as you stay ignorant of the things of God. The scriptures talks about the *"...The rulers of the darkness of this world..."* As a believer you cannot afford to live your life in ignorance of spiritual things.

We must be established in the truth of God's word in order for us to have a triumphant life. The level of triumph in our lives will be determined by our depth in the truth. Having a big Bible is not the same as knowing what is written in it. In the conflict of life what prevails is not the word written black and white in the Bible but the one written on the tablets of our hearts.

To be established in the truth means the following:

1. We already know the truth. You cannot be established in what you don't know.* How can you use what you don't know exist? We can have money in our wallet and still stay hungry if you don't know that the money is there.

2. The truth must have become a personal conviction in our lives.* Not just because we heard it said in Church. It has to be something we cannot doubt again even when all we see around us is contrary to what the truth says.

3. The word of God is the truth. Everything else is a fact.* The medical report is a fact, not the truth. That someone is jobless today is a fact not the truth. Established in the truth means you can separate the fact from the truth. If you are not established in the truth the lies of the devil will get you.

CONFESSION:

I will not consider the circumstances of life. I will focus on the truth of God's word and be established in it.

LEARN MORE: John 8:32; 17:17, Rom 4:17-21

PRAYER REQUEST: In the name of Jesus we decree that the sanctifying power of the word will be at work again today as the people read Inspiration. John 17:17

Inspiring men!

A true father does not only provide sperm and money; he provides wisdom, direction and protection for his family. BE A MAN!"

Inspiring men!

*What a man does may be personal but never private. What he does may be secret but will eventually show up in his generations after him. The man is the door of entry into generations. (Lord have mercy on us)

HIGH PLACES

———— ∞∞ ————

Text: "He market my feet like hinds' feet, and setteth me upon my high places." Psalm 18:33

Let's begin today by saying that there are "low places" of life. This is a description of a life that is far below what God planned and intended for us. The "low places" is also a description of a life that robs us of the glory of God. Everything about your life should bring glory and honor to God. People around you should look at your life and thank God for the things they see in your life.

Whatever is contrary to the glory of God in our lives is an experience of the "low places". By the authority in the name of Jesus I decree your relocation from the "low places" to the "high places."

We were born for the high places. I want you to note that the word "place" in our anchor scripture is pluralized. "Places" means every area of our lives. That is God's intention for us. Your high place is the description of having the best of God and becoming the best of God in every area of our lives. I believe that life is progressive and in phases, but at the same time I also believe that at whatever phase we are right now we should be the best at that phase. As other phase of life unfolds we should also be the best at that phase. Don't postpone the best days of your life until when you get married. Even as a single guy or lady walk upon you high places at this stage of your life. Don't wait until you graduate from school; walk on your high places right now. Be the best and have the best of God right now at this stage of your life. I see God setting you upon your high places in 2020. You will have the best and become the best this year.

The description of your life this year will be an exact description of the glory of God. Don't allow anything to hold you down; you were born for the "high places."

PRAYER:

I declare that my feet are set upon my high places in every area of my life this year. Every journey to the low places is forbidden this year.

LEARN MORE: Isa 60:1-2

DIVINE APPOINTMENT

⸺∞⸻

Text: "Whereunto I am appointed a preacher, and an apostle, and a teacher of the Gentiles." 2 Tim 1:11

There is so much lobbying and scheming going on in the corridors of power to secure political appointments. Many people can go to any length to secure appointments in multinational companies. This is basically because there are so much financial gains associated with such appointments. As good and powerful as these appointments are they are temporary. There is no political office that is forever. They all have a shelf life. The gains of these appointments are limited to this natural sphere of life.

In our anchor scriptures today apostle Paul was talking about a different kind of appointment. He was talking about a divine appointment that did not derive its origin from the political powers that be. It was not a product of well written curriculum vitae to a multinational company. This was a divine appointment from God. By inference I believe that there is a divine appointment on the life of every believer. We may never have realized this before but there is a divine appointment on your life even before you were born. Locating divine appointment and walking in it will bring the highest gain in your life. The worth of a divine assignment is far greater than the appointments of this world.

Before Paul located the divine appointment on his life he was a lawyer of repute. He was highly respected among his contemporaries. As soon as he found divine appointment everything else did not matter to him again. The impact and the influence of his life became so outstanding as soon as he settled within the confines of divine appointment. Don't stop at just been a civil servant, a tailor, a lawyer, a political office holder – go further to locate God's appointment on your life.

CONFESSION:

There is a divine appointment on my life. I was crafted and equipped with a divine mandate even before I was born.

LEARN MORE: Jer 1:5

PRAYER REQUEST: We declare clarity of direction and purpose for everyone reading Inspiration. Eph 1:17-18

Inspiring Men!

*"A woman shared the brief teaching on Inspiring Men with her husband and he became very angry. Some men have also blocked my line on whatsapp. The ability to receive the truth and be corrected by it is a major sign of humility. Pride has never taken anyone far. Each truth I share are truths God is dealing with me in my personal life. Truth embraced is deliverance embraced. Truth ignored is bondage activated.

NEVER ASHAMED

∽∾∿

Text: "For I am not ashamed of the gospel of Christ: for it is the power of God unto salvation to everyone that believed....." Rom 1:16

A shame driven life is a life in which you are not proud of certain aspects of your life. Living this way produces weakness in our lives and ineffectiveness in functioning at the highest level of life that God designed for us. The direct opposite of been ashamed is been confident about life and about yourself.

I want to share with you today some things you must never be ashamed of.

1. Never be ashamed of your union with Christ - If you are ashamed of this you have automatically reduce your effectiveness as a believer. How will you communicate what you are not proud of to someone else? The gospel of Christ is the greatest privilege of life. If you are saved it means divinity has come to take residence in your life. It means that the power of God has been given to you to become everything you were created to be. Why will you be ashamed of this? What you have in Christ is the answer and the cure to every human problem.

2. Never be ashamed of your difference - God is a God of difference. He made each one of us unique and different. If he wanted you to be like someone else he would have made you exactly like them. He made you different so that you can fulfil his unique plan and purpose for your life. Similarities create conflicts, while difference creates significance. One of the greatest breakthroughs in forensic science is based on the difference created by God in each one of us. This is why thumb prints can be used to locate people. Please celebrate your difference. You may not be able to do what someone else is doing. But you can do something that others cannot do. Discover your difference, celebrate it and develop it. Other people will be drawn to you.

PRAYER:

Thank you Lord for making me so different. Thank you for the uniqueness in my life.

LEARN MORE: Ps 139:13-18

PRAYER REQUEST: Lord cause your presence to accompany the daily reading of your word through Inspiration. Mark 16:20

PRAYING FOR PRISONERS:

Please join me daily!

Lord we decree a fresh manifestation of your presence to prisoners in their cells across the nations today. Heb 13:5-6

Fellow citizens of the world,

I address you today as the globe is shaking, the kings and rulers of the earth have now known that they are but mere men.

A mere virus have emptied the streets of proud cities. National and international Airlines have been grounded, schools closed, entertainment events closed, even friendly hand shakes are now avoided to elbow shakes.

Have you paused and wondered what is really happening. Why is there so much global panic now.

The thing is, GOD is trying to get the attention of the world. It looks like a final warning from the office of the CEO of the UNIVERSE.

It is a signal that a very big event is about to take place in the globe.

God never does anything without first giving out warnings to alert humanity.

JESUS CHRIST is COMING SOON from the SKIES and all GLOBAL TV networks will carry it live with commentaries of the event. Revelation 1:7 Matthew 24:29-31

The world will be divided into two groups of people.

*Those who made the rapture and left the earth to be with Jesus Christ in the sky.

*Those who never believed in Jesus Christ before the rapture and they cannot be saved again because the Holy Spirit will not be there to convict them of sin to repent and be saved.

Now, come to think of it, Just a mere Virus and the whole Earth is on Panic mode.

Just a Virus and Businesses are shutting down and streets of cities like London are empty.

Just a Virus and Citizens of nations cannot Move around the way they wish to and all flights from Europe to America are shut down.

Just a Virus, and the nations we look to as developed nations are being Threatened without bombs.

Just a Virus, Educational institutions are closed and entertainment centers are closed.

Just a Virus and Religious sites are closed and Churches are announcing no services till further notice.

Just a Virus, and the world market is collapsing and nations are entering into recession with speed.

If an Ordinary Virus could do all these, Imagine what will Be on this Earth, the day King Jesus Christ will return in the sky.

Take note, when Jesus Christ appears in the sky, all cars, trucks, air planes, trains and ships driven by prepared saints will have the drivers and pilots ejected by the power of Jesus Christ in the rapture into the sky. And that will cause the greatest Crashes of air, road, rail and sea ever. It is a day of gloom and doom.

May GOD! Give Us Understanding to know what is about to Happen to those who will not be raptured on that day.

Corona is a warning alert from heaven to the whole world saying that something of heavy global magnitude is about to happen.

Sir/Ma, brothers/sisters, Make use of this moment by Repenting from Sin and Accepting JESUS CHRIST as Lord and Savior before it is too late.

2nd Corinthians 6:1-2
The Door of Mercy is About to Be Closed finally. It is a fearful thing to think that a man will be lost forever into eternity in a burning hell with brimstone and Sulphur when he or she could have just stopped to pray now and accept Jesus Christ as Lord and Savior. If you have

read this and you are not sure if you are born again, then I urge you to pray now like this:

Dear heavenly, I come to you as a sinner and I am very sorry for all my sins. I believe today that Jesus Christ died for my sins and I confess with my mouth that Jesus Christ is Lord and I belive in my heart that God raised Him from the dead. Write my name in the book of life and cancel my name from the book of death. I confess I am saved. Amen."

Please do it now and be saved.

Please SHARE urgently and save a soul from hell and free your hand from their blood.

ABANDONED BY MEN

Text: "Even if my father and mother abandon me, the Lord will hold me close." Ps 27:10 (NLT)

We all grew up in one form of human family or another. This is where we all receive the initial support that was required to move up in life. In well-structured families these supports remain available one way or another all our lives. The support could be moral, financial, spiritual etc. Joseph also had such a support at the initial stage of his life, along the line this support was withdrawn from him. He was abandoned by his brothers who would have supplied the greatest support he needed to move into God's dreams for his life. He was sold into the house of Potiphar to serve as a servant, he was fortunate enough to have some levels of support from his master. The events unfolded in the house of Potiphar that landed him in trouble. This support again was withdrawn. He was abandoned by his master in the Prison.

These were different levels of been abandoned by men in the life of Joseph. As the story revealed even though he was abandoned by men he was not abandoned by God. We must never confuse the two together. Though human supports were gone divine support was intact. This was all Joseph needed to become God's dream for him. As long as God's support is still available He will ensure that what we need is supplied from unexpected places. Who would have thought that Joseph will meet in the Prison someone who will introduce him to the throne?

This is what David was talking about in our anchor scripture today. The best of human relationships are channels and not source. When a channel is blocked the source remains forever. God is our only source. Get your eyes fixed on God this year. He will never leave you nor forsake you.

PRAYER:

Thank you Lord because you are my inexhaustible source. My eyes are fixed on you this year. I repent of every way I might have depended on men in the past.

LEARN MORE: Ps 121:1-2

PRAYER REQUEST: Lord open the eyes of understanding of your people as they read your word again today. Psalm 119:18

LIVING IN THE PAS

—— ∞∞ ——

Text: "Remember ye not the former things, neither consider te things of old. Behold, I will do a new thing..." Isa 43:18-19

Living in the past is like trying to maintain a relationship with a dead person by keeping their corpse in your bedroom. There is no amount of communication that makes sense again with them. They are gone and gone forever. The past is gone. Whatever happened in the past could become a stumbling block for us today if we refuse to let go of it.

The heart breaks, the disappointments and the losses of the past should be left in the past. If you have survived them then it means that today of your life is what matter now.

The sins and the mistakes of the past are forgiven in Christ. His blood was all that was needed to wash them off. As far as God is concerned once a man is born again the past is completely dealt with. The Bible tells us that our sins and iniquities he will remember no more. The blood of Jesus paid for our sins, there is no point trying to pay again for it by staying guilty.

The disappointment of the past does not define the possibilities of today. The past could develop a mental stronghold for us that keep holding us back from moving forward in life. If we are not careful we can develop a mind-set that keeps expecting what happened in the past to keep happening again. Expectations become realities. So many people are in self imposed prisons in their minds. Break that prison gate now and set yourself free.

2019 is gone and gone forever, leave the hurts and the disappointments behind and reach forth to the new things God is doing in your life today. I see God doing a new thing in your life today, I see God sending your way new opportunities and fresh open doors. Let the doors of your expectations be opened again.

*CONFESSION:

The past has no hold on my life again. I am completely free from the hurts and the disappointments.

LEARN MORE: Isa 43:19, Heb 8:12

PRAYER REQUEST: Lord for everyone who are just newly introduced to Inspiration we decree a lifetime encounter for them. 2 Cor 3:18

Inspiring Men!

"One of the most difficult thing to do as human is to forgive. But learning to do it is liberating. It frees our souls to soar. If your heart is truly full of the love of God and you understand how much God had forgiven you then it will be a pleasure to let go of any offence at any level. Release yourself from the bondage of unforgivness" BE A MAN!

: *PRAYING FOR PRISONERS:*

Please join me daily!

Lord for everyone who have become hopeless in prison we decree a supernatural restoration of hope. Col 1:27

DEVELOPED
HUMAN SPIRIT

Text: "And now, brethren, I commend you to God, and to the word of his grace, which is able to build to build you up..." Acts 20:32

The human spirit is also referred to as the inner man, the spirit man or the hidden man of the heart. These phrases are used in different places all over scriptures. When we got born again it was this part of us that actually became a new creature. The other two parts of the three parts of man are the soul and the body. At new birth the soul and the body did not change. The soul is made up of the mind, the will and the emotions.

If the soul and the body are allowed to control our lives independent of the recreated spirit then there will be a problem. The mind also needs to be renewed in other for it to cooperate with the recreated human spirit. An un-renewed mind will oppose what God is bringing forth through our spirit. However for the recreated human spirit to be strong it has to be developed. The extent to which this has taken place is the extent to which it could take charge and control what goes on in the other parts of man. The body actually is like a messenger that carries out the instructions it receives from the soul and the spirit. When there are no signals from the inner man the body does whatever it likes to satisfy itself.

#The human spirit is developed when it's constantly fed with the word of God.

The word of God is able to build us up and put us in charge of the frailties of the human flesh. We are all weak in one area of our lives or the other; it's the development of our spirit man that puts us over such weaknesses. We could be so developed that such weaknesses will no longer be part of our lives.

"Constantly praying in the Spirit also builds us up on our most holy faith.

Developing your human spirit is purely your personal responsibility. If you don't do it, it will remain undone and you will suffer its consequence.

CONFESSION:

The word of God is building me up daily within as I read and listen to the word. I am growing within.

LEARN MORE: 2 Corinth 4:16, Jude 20

PRAYER REQUEST: Lord cause the fire of your Spirit consume afresh everyone reading Inspiration. Rom 12:11

CREATIVE MINDS

*Text: "In the beginning God created the heaven and the earth."
Gen 1:1*

The world was empty, void and filled with chaos. The creative mind of God came to put orderliness into the disorderliness that God saw. Out of chaos God brought orderliness. Out of ugliness God brought beauty. Out of emptiness God brought fullness. That was the creative mind at work.

God has created us in his image and likeness so that we can also be creative like him. Whatever state of life you find yourself don't be hopeless, we can come out of it. Built into us is the mind of Christ to bring into existence and bring to reality what has not been before. Whenever we find ourselves in a tight corner or in a dead end the creative mind of God in us comes into play to create a way out for us.

The creative mind is a major deposit of divinity in us to make the most of our lives. God filled Bazaleel with a creative mind by the Spirit to devise designs that have never been before. In whatever field of life we find ourselves this creative mind can come to bear. As a fashion designer the creative mind will create styles that no other tailor in town can design. These designs will be unique to you. The creative mind will help those of us in ministry to touch lives in a way that no one ever thought about before. The creative mind of God in a surgeon could help him out to do surgery in a way that beats human imagination. A teacher operating with a creative mind will teach his or her students in a way that they will perfectly understand.

The creative mind at work in us will help us not to be normal but different and unique. This will help us to stand out in the crowd of life. If you are going to excel in this world you must be different and extraordinary. This will be possible by the operation of the Spirit of God in us, helping us to be creative.

DECLARATION:

The mind of Christ is at work in me. My mind is creative. My mind provides answers and solutions.

LEARN MORE: Exo 31:2-5, 1 Corinth 2:16

PRAYER REQUEST; Lord by your Spirit revive the prayer life of everyone reading Inspiration. Luke 18:1

[6/16/2019, 11:25 AM] +234 813 850 8568: *INSPIRATION*

LAW OF RECOGNITION 1

━━━∞∞∞━━━

Text: "Is not this the carpenter's son? Is not his mother called Mary? And his brethren, James, and Jose ...are they not all with us...?" Matt 13:55-56

A couple became obsessed with the pursuit of gold during the great gold rush of the late 1800's. They decided to sell their farm and everything owned to go in search of gold. Failure after failure they ended up bankrupt in Europe. After many years, they decided to come back to America and visit their farm. However when they arrived they could not get close to their farm because it was surrounded with security guards and surveillance equipment to protect it. It turned out that under their farmhouse was the second largest gold reserve in America, now controlled by the Government. The farm they sold to go search for gold held the largest gold mine in North America. They simply did not recognize it.

Everything you need in life is already in your life merely awaiting your recognition of it. What you need you already have, all that needs to happen is for you to recognize them. Opportunities, miracles, breakthroughs pass us everyday unrecognized.

Anything you refuse to recognize will exit your life – a gift, a person or a miracle.

There are doors that God has opened for us that we just refuse to recognize them. Jesus came as the savior, the healer, the way maker etc but the Jews did not recognize him. Even up till now some of them are still waiting for the Messiah to come. What a tragic loss. They only saw him as the carpenter son. Only God knows how many opportunities we have missed in life. The two thieves that were crucified with Jesus on the cross ended up in different places because one recognized the divine moment and Christ crucified along with them. The other was so blinded to that divine opportunity to make right his eternal destiny. I pray for you today that your eyes will open to recognize opportunities.

CONFESSION:

The eyes of my understanding are opened to recognise opportunities. I see clearly miracles lined up in my path daily and I take full advantage of them.

LEARN MORE: Luke 23:39-43, Eph 1:17-18

PRAYER REQUEST: Lord we declare that the eyes of your people are opened as they read your word in Inspiration again today. Eph 1:17-18

LAW OF RECOGNITION 2

———— ∞∞∞ ————

Text: "And every one that was in distress, and every one that was in debt, and every one that was discontented, gathered themselves unto him; and he became captain over them..." 1 Sam 22:2

What you refuse to recognise will slip through your life. It therefore becomes necessary to increase the rate at which we can recognise opportunities knocking at our doors. It takes more than the natural eyes to see opportunities. We need the eyes of the Spirit to see clearly. Opportunities come disguised most times.

The rough edges in people may make you think there is nothing good that may come out of them. If you look at people merely based on how they look outwardly you will miss so many potential people that God will send your way. This group of men in our anchor scripture gathered themselves to David. At this point they did not have anything to offer David. He could have despised them and send them away. These men were distressed, in debt and discontented. At the end of the day these men became the "mighty men" of David. They were the ones God used to fight the major battles for David. If he had not recognised potentials in them he would have missed out on what God packaged in them for his advantage.

Please recognise the grace of God on people. Stop judging people based on their mere outward appearance. Built into their spirit are great potentials for something extraordinary. This applies to each one of us too. Recognise the grace of God in your life. Recognise the potentials that God has placed within your spirit. Where you are and what you have done so far does not define the limits of your life. We belong to a limitless God. There is no limit to how far we can go in life.

Jesse did not recognise that his son David had the potential of becoming a King. That was why he was not even invited in the first place to be tested. Please don't despise people. You will be despising someone that God made in his image. Please recognise value in your spouse, your friends, your neighbours etc.

PRAYER:

Lord I repent of every way I have despised people in the past. I receive grace to recognise value in people.

LEARN MORE: 1 Sam 16:6-13, 2 Sam 23:8-13

PRAYER REQUEST: Lord cause your Spirit to draw the hearts of your people daily to spend time with you. Prov 8:34

RECOGNISING DIVINE MOMENTS

~~~~~~

Text: "For who hath despised the day of small things?..." Zech 4:10

About eight years ago I discovered that I was sending free texts on my phone. So I took advantage of that privilege to start sending Inspiring text messages to our Church members. So many people were blessed by it. Along the line a brother in church introduced to me the need to use bulk SMS to reach church members. It was not really embraced by the Church I was then but I saw it as another tool to reach out to people. Personally I started paying the Brother to help me send bulk SMS to people. I started collecting phone numbers everywhere I go. At a point I had over one thousand people on my list. The brother asked me one day what name we'll give to the text as it should appear on people's phones, I found myself saying "Inspiration", and this was how we came about "Inspiration". For me these were divine moments. At a particular time I had a message by Pastor Faith Oyedepo on diligence and I felt Inspired to start writing daily devotionals. Now I looked back and I thank God for helping me to recognise these divine moments.

Divine moments are destiny moulding moments in our lives that God opens a new chapter in our lives. These are times in our lives that God brings our way people that are going to make major contributions in our lives. We all need such moments to fulfil destiny. God will also orchestrate such moments. But we must be sensitive. We must be open to recognise such divine moments. If you are going to recognise divine moments then you must never treat anything as common or small. A small door that God opens today may lead to a wider door in your life. A small opening today may lead to wider openings tomorrow. But if you refuse to walk through the small opening because of its size you will miss the greater doors. The days of little beginnings will lead to greater endings. The seemingly small divine moments I explained to you earlier has helped us to touch thousands of lives for exactly six years now.

PRAYER:

Lord help me to be sensitive to divine moments in the coming year. I overcome every spiritual blindness.

LEARN MORE: Job 8:7

PRAYER REQUEST: Lord grant everyone reading Inspiration an understanding heart to produce a 100-fold of the word. Matt 13:23

RECOGNISING THE SEASONS OF LIFE

---◦∞◦---

Text: "...The Children of Issachar, which were men that had understanding of the times, to know what Israel ought to do...." 1 Chron 12:32

Life is in seasons. The understanding and the recognition of season will make a major difference in our lives. If you fail to recognise the seasons of life you will miss out on so many things. The sons of Issachar were in control because they recognised season that others failed to recognise.

Recognising seasons will help you to achieve the following:

1. It will help you to do the right thing at the right time.*

2. It will help you to get the best out of life when the chances are brightest.*

3. It will ensure that we reach out for the best God has in store for us on time.* Time Wastibg things are eliminated out of our lives.

Seasons simply means time intervals in nature. Every wise farmer understands this principle. Every crop that will do well has the right season for it to do so. Maize planted at the wrong season may produce some seeds but will not produce as much as if it was planted at the right time. When it is planted at the right season the forces of nature such as rain also comes in to help in its maximum yield.

There is a right season to go to school and earn a degree. There have been cases of people who earned degrees at a very old age but this is very few. The best time to do it is when your mind is still fresh to absorb information and you are still strong to go through the rigour of the academic life. The best time to start serving God and discover his purpose for your life is when you are still young. The scriptures tell us to remember God in the days of our youth. This implies that the "days of our Youth" is the best season to invest everything we are in God. If you don't recognise the seasons of your life you will waste them.

CONFESSION:

I have an understanding of times. I know exactly what to do with my life per time. I have precision in life.

LEARN MORE: Ecc 3:1-11; 12:1-2

PRAYER REQUEST: Lord we ask that the steps of everyone reading Inspiration are ordered in the path of destiny.

RECOGNISING WHO YOU ARE

—⦿—

Text: "That the communication of your faith may become effectual by the acknowledging of every good thing which is in you in Christ Jesus." Philemon 6

If you don't recognise who you are the Devil will tell you who you are not. The circumstances of life will also paint a wrong picture of who you are. When you have a wrong picture of yourself it will produce wrong outcomes in your life. It will be difficult to make a head way in life when we have a wrong perspectives of ourselves. The Devil actually specialises in giving us a distorted picture of our worth and value.

One major relevance of the word of God is that it gives us the right picture of our worth and value. There are other people who may come along to help us see worth and values in ourselves, but that will be grossly inadequate to live on in this turbulent world. We must see value and worth for ourselves.

If you have ever failed before it may paint a picture of you as a failure. That is what circumstances says, not what God says. What happened to you or what did not happen to you does not define who you are. You have to be resolute not to accept whatever is contrary to what God says about you.

Recognise that you are the best of your type that God ever made. You are not in any way inferior to anyone. God never made anyone second class. You are first class all the way. This is not arrogance but a humble submission to what God already made you. No matter what your grades are in school you are still first class all the way. The Spirit of God dwells in you and that makes you extraordinary. Can you recognise this? The picture you have of yourself will determine the future you'll experience. The experiences of your life will first be painted on the tablets of your heart. Just as an Architect draws the picture of a future house so also you are painting the picture of your future by what you think of yourself. You are the child of a King; you are limitless.

CONFESSION:

I am a child of a King. The royal blood flows in me. I am not inferior to anyone. Am the best of my type.

LEARN MORE: 1 Pet 2:9

PRAYER REQUEST: Lord sanctify the heart of your people as they read your word in Inspiration daily. John 17:17

PRODIGAL LIVING

———— ⚬⚬⚬ ————

Text: "And not many days after the younger son gathered all together, and took his journey into a far country, and there wasted his substance with riotous living." Luke 15:13

I don't know how old you are right now but I want you to do an audit of your life today and see what you have done with all the privileges and opportunities that life has given you. Take a look at how you handled the privileges and the opportunities God brought your way so far this year.

It was not completely wrong that the prodigal son asked his father for his own portion of inheritance. It must have been an acceptable practice in that culture then. It was an opportunity for him to start building his own life and destiny. It was more or less his father giving him the seeds to cultivate his future harvest. What went wrong was that he spent his inheritance on riotous living. The seeds he would have planted or invested were consumed. If he had gone to invest his inheritance nobody would have blamed him.

Prodigal living is when we waste and throw away the privileges that God brings our way in life. The failure of the prodigal son was that he did not recognise that what he had was a seed. Just as we said a couple of days ago whatever you don't recognise you will eventually lose. Only God knows how much precious time we have wasted this year doing what never added any value to our lives. A man or woman is prodigal when they waste opportunities, time, energy and resources.

The beauty of this is that the prodigal son came back home and received the mercy of the father. As we step into the second half of 2019 be determined to make the best use of the remaining part of the year

PRAYER:

Lord by the help of your Spirit every form of prodigal living comes to an end in my life. I receive grace to make the best use of every opportunity that will come my way daily.

LEARN MORE: Heb 4:16

PRAYER REQUEST: We declare that Christ will be formed in the heart of everyone reading Inspiration. Gal 4:19

WORK IN PROGRESS

———∞∞∞———

Text: "But he knoweth the way that I take; when he hath tried me, I shall come forth as gold." Job 23:10

The process of taking the gold through the fire by a goldsmith is not to destroy it. But rather to bring out a high quality gold. Gold in its raw form has very little or no value. The purifying process brings out its worth and value.

I agree with you that life could take us through circumstances that are not palatable. Looking at them through the eye of faith we'll understand that these are purifying process of life. This is a process that is designed to bring out the best in our lives, so that we can be the best God created us for. God is working behind the scenes of our lives in the midst of the circumstances of life. While Joseph was going through his experience in Potiphar's house and in the prison God was at work, ordering his steps to the throne. Behind the scene of the tragic experience of Job God was working to bring double restoration in his life. Just as we have learned before these experiences were not caused by God but God used them for his glory.

Every day as you wake up I want you to understand that divine work is in progress in your life. The ending of a day, week, month or year is not the end of God's plans for your life. Years come and years go, but divine purpose and plans remains the same. If there is what will happen God's plans and purpose for your life will find a clearer and greater expressions on a daily basis. There could be expectations that are not yet met but work is still in progress. Disappointments did not stop divine program in your life. I want to inspire you to see beyond the setbacks and the breakdowns. In God's program they are raw materials for his ultimate program for our lives. Joseph's setbacks eventually took him to his ultimate destiny.

CONFESSION:

Divine work is in progress in my life. God is behind the scenes of my life. Every day will bring a clearer and greater expression of God's plans and purpose for me.

LEARN MORE: Rom 8:28

PRAYER REQUEST: Lord we ask for fresh oil over the lives of everyone reading Inspiration to be continually on fire for you. Psalm 92:10

EVERLASTING ARMS

Text: "The eternal God is thy refuge, and underneath are the everlasting arms; and he shall thrust out the enemy from before thee; and shall say, Destroy them." Deut 33:27

The life of a child is so simple. The child has no cares or worries. The child has so much confidence in the parents. The child is not wondering how his school fees will be paid or where the next meal will come from. The child knows that Daddy will figure that out. Underneath the child are the arms of the parents. This is not just talking of physical arms, but arms of provision, arms of constant supply. Arms of protection. We talk of sleeping like a baby; this is a description of a carefree life of a baby.

The arms of God are not limited to a particular day, month or year, it is an everlasting arm. We can rest like a baby in these arms, trusting God to take care of every aspect of our lives on a daily basis.

Anxiety is eliminated when we understand that God is mindful of us. He has all the details of our lives right from conception to our old age. Every minute is covered, every hour is secured, every day is sure, and every month is perfected. Anxiety is a direct opposite of a heart trusting in the faithfulness of God. Anxiety is like trying to figure out how the bones are been formed in the womb. It's really of no use. We cannot change anything with anxiety. It's a waste of energy.

God has gone ahead of us into tomorrow. The angels are already positioned on every road we'll pass on daily basis. The standard of the Spirit is already raised against every weapon that may be formed against us. The arms of God are positioned to carry you all through your life time.

PRAYER:

Thank you Lord for the everlasting arms that are positioned to carry me through life. Thank you for going ahead of me into my tomorrow.

GOD OF ABRAHAM, ISAAC AND JACOB

———— ⌘ ————

Text: "Moreover he said, I am the God of thy father, the God of Abraham, the God of Isaac, and the God of Jacob. And Moses hid his face; for he was afraid to look upon God."Ex 3:6

God was introducing Moses to his destiny. This was an assignment that was bigger than everything he had ever done. He had been just a mere shepherd leading sheep. But now he was going to confront the most powerful king on the face of the earth at that time. He was going to lead millions of people out of bondage into the Promised Land. This was far bigger than his experience and expertise. God had to first of all help him to appreciate who was behind him.

God did this by helping him to appreciate that He was the same God that helped his father; Abraham, Isaac and Jacob. This was an assurance that the same help that was available to his father will be available for him too.

Abraham came out of his kindred and became extremely successful. God led him on several occasions to make him a giant on the earth. God fulfilled in his life one of the greatest promises made personally to a man. Isaac became prosperous in a strange land that was plagued with famine. In the midst of this drought he reaped a hundred-fold;

he went forward until he became very great. Jacob was also mightily helped. His father-in-law cheated him several times until God intervened for him. Eventually God met with him to change his name. God was telling Moses that if I could help these people I will equally help you. . Moses went on to face Pharaoh with this assurance and confidence.

In whatever way we desire His help it will be available for us. He did not fail Abraham, Isaac and Jacob. He will not fail you in in life.

CONFESSION:

The God of Abraham, Isaac and Jacob is my God. Just as they were helped I will also be helped in life. God has never failed before and he will not fail in my case

LEARN MORE: Ex 2:24, Gen 26:1-14, Isa 41:10-16

PRAYER REQUEST: Lord we ask that the fire of commitment to God will burn afresh in the lives of everyone reading Inspiration. Lev 6:12

A GUIDE UNTO DEATH

Text: "For this God is our God forever and ever: he will be our guide even unto death."Ps 48:14

God's commitments on our lives are not seasonal. His promise is to carry us unto hoary hairs, to an old age. Whatever stage and seasons of life we find ourselves God is committed to our lives there.

God is committed to leading and guiding us for the rest of our lives. On a daily basis God is ready to guide us into where His blessings are waiting for us. For this to become a reality in our lives we must also be committed to following his guidance for our lives. The plans and purpose of God for our lives will only become a reality only to the extent to which we follow his guidance for our lives. None of us can ever outgrow the need to be divinely guided by God. Each one of us must renew our commitment to follow divine guidance in daily.

We must understand that God is a God of new beginnings. The change of the dates on a daily basis is not what will make things new. It's the renewed commitment we have to follow divine guidance that will produce new things in our lives. The path we follow yesterday may not necessarily be the same path we'll follow today. We must learn to ask God questions concerning our lives. Some of us may have to make major changes in our lives. These principles are all over scripture. Abraham was already an old man at the age of seventy five, but God had to change his location to bring to pass his promises on his life. God insisted that Isaac remain where he was though he made an attempt to relocate to where he felt was a greener pasture.

Today seek God's direction before you set out on any project or trip. A right step taken at the right time will make a huge difference in your life on a daily basis.

ENQUIRY:

Lord what is your plans and purpose for me today. What path should I follow today? What changes should I make in my life today?

LEARN MORE: Ps 23:1-6

PRAYER REQUEST: Lord cause your word to heal and deliver as the people read Inspiration daily. Psalm 107:20

POWER OF EXPECTATION

∽∾∽

Text: "For surely there is an end; and thine expectation shall not be cut off." Prov 23:18

The Woman with the issue of blood was sick for so many years-twelve long years. She has done everything medically possible to get out of that situation. Every effort proved abortive. She had spent all she had on the problem. Instead of improving it was getting worse.

If you read the story carefully we'll see that she did not really lost all hope of receiving an answer. She kept taking steps to get her problem resolved. When she heard of Jesus her expectation rose up again. If she had given up on her condition she would not have taken the steps she took. Expectation keeps your "antenna", waiting to see your miracle show up. As long as you are breathing you cannot give up on what God says about you. If it is written in the word of God you must hold on to your expectation until it becomes a reality in your life. It took the woman with the issue of blood twelve year to come out of her situation. It was her expectation that kept her on. She might have died before meeting Jesus.

Job in the midst of his challenge said "...All the days of my appointed time will I hold on to my expectation, till my change come."(Paraphrased) Job 14:14b. This man lost everything all in one day but he did not lose his expectations. When you lose your expectation you have lost the possibility of a favorable outcome. This was why the latter days of Job were better than his beginning. Everything he lost was restored twice back to him. I see a major restoration taking place in your life today. Refuse to give up on God's plan for your life. Expectations keep you on and open to what God is ready to bring forth in your life.

CONFESSION:

I will hold on to my expectations until God's plans come to pass in my life. I will not give up on what God has said concerning me.

LEARN MORE: Mark 5:25-29, Romans 4:17-21

PRAYER REQUEST: Lord cause everyone reading Inspiration to take root downwards and bear fruit upward spiritually. Isa 37:31

INCREASING STRENGHT

Text: "A wise man is strong; yea, a man of knowledge increaseth strength." Prov 24:5

Strength in the scripture above is not referring to physical strength. What you'll need for physical strength will merely be good diet at the right time, regular physical exercise and regular rest.

Strength here refers to the ability to handle the issues of our lives. It talks about the capacity to face the circumstances of life. It has nothing to do with how big you are or how tall you are. King Saul was said to be the tallest man in Israel. He was physically qualified to have faced Goliath, but he could. David was young, inexperienced but he had an unusual inner strength to face the challenge on ground. The strength we are referring to here is inner strength.

Knowledge increases our strength to handle issues. Whatever you are ignorant about you will be weak about. Knowledge increases our ability to be more productive and resourceful.

David had the knowledge of the covenant. He knew that the uncircumcised Philistine should not be a threat to the circumcised armies of the living God. In the New Testament language he knew that the greater one living in him was greater than the gods of the Philistines.

The greater your knowledge of God the stronger you become in the face of contrary situations. "...but the people that do know their God shall be strong, and do exploits." Daniel 11:32b. The exploits we experience in life will be in direct proportion to our knowledge of God. Take conscious steps to increase your knowledge of God in that area of your challenge. Don't just fold your arm to say "whatever will be will be" that is a language of mediocre. Whatever will be is up to you. Up to your knowledge of God.

CONFESSION:

I am filled with the knowledge of God's will in all wisdom and spiritual understanding. I am increasing in the knowledge of God.

LEARN MORE: Prov 24:10, Col 1:9-10

PRAYER REQUEST: Lord cause everyone reading your word through Inspiration to be addicted to living by your word. Matt 4:4

RULE OVER
YOUR SPIRIT

—◦◦◦—

Text: "He that hath no rule over his own spirit is like a city that is broken down, and without walls." Prov 25:28

In the ancient times the major form of protections in cities are fortified walls. Wars were quite rampant in those days. One Kingdom is always fighting against another kingdom, which made the walls absolutely necessary. Once the walls are broken down, it becomes so easy for the intruding enemy to gain easy access.

The walls are for the following reasons:

1. To protect the territorial boundaries of the city.*

2. To protect the intruders from gaining entrance.*

A City with a broken down walls is open, vulnerable and exposed to everything that can go wrong. This is the exact description of a life that has no rule over his spirit. The word 'rule' here means self control.

Lack of self control could be expressed in various forms: This could express itself in lack of self control over the use of our time. Time is precious; if we lose control over time we've lost control over life itself. Time management is life management. We don't have all the time in the world to do everything. We only have enough time to do what is relevant and productive for us. But when we fail to do this we'll end up spending our God given precious time on irrelevant and unproductive ventures.

Lack of self control could also be expressed in lack of control over our appetite, sleep, sexual drive and the rest. Whichever one it is, such a life is open, exposed and vulnerable to every wrong intruders.

Self-Control is an internal work of the Holy Spirit within us as we yield ourselves to his dealings and promptings within us. This will protect your life.

CONFESSION:

There is control over my spirit. I am internally controlled by the Holy Spirit. Intruders are helpless. I have control over my time, my appetite and my sexual drive.

LEARN MORE: Gal 5:22-23

PRAYER REQUEST: Lord cause the eyes of your people to be open to behold wondrous things out of your word daily. Psalm 119:18

SPIRITUAL MIRROR 1

—————∞∞∞—————

Text: "For if any be a hearer of the word, and not a doer, he is like unto a man beholding his natural face in a glass (mirror)." James 1:23

In order for us to understand the place of the word of God in our lives several symbols are used all over scripture to help our understanding. Symbols like hammer, lamp, water, mirror etc. are used to paint the pictures for us.

The word of God from our opening verse is a spiritual glass or mirror. Virtually all of us use mirror daily. It has become a natural part of us. Ladies have it handy in their bags virtually everywhere they go. I strongly believe that's how God wants us to relate with his word daily. Something we carry in our hearts everywhere we go and we refer to on a continuous basis.

The mirror serves two major purpose:

1. It helps us to see what we look like.*

2. It helps us to make adjustments where required.*

This is also a picture of the role of the word of God in our lives. The word of God shows us our real picture from God's perspective. No matter what the situations look like in the natural the word of God as a spiritual mirror shows us what we look like from God's perspective. Abraham saw himself initially as childless but God saw him as a father of many nations. Moses saw himself from the natural mirror or perspective as someone that was slow of speech and could not talk. God saw him as a god unto Pharaoh.

You can't do great things in life if all you see and know about yourself are natural limitations. You can't go beyond what you see and say about yourself. We must look intently at the spiritual mirror and accept the divine perspectives over our lives.

DECLARATION:

I accept the picture that God's word paint about me. Whatever God's word say about me is what is real and final.

LEARN MORE: James 1:23-25, 2 Cor 3:18

PRAYER REQUEST: Lord cause your word to purify the earth of your people through Inspiration to be worthy vessels to carry your purpose. 2 Tim 2:19

FED BY THE WORD

———⚬∞⚬———

Text: "Till I come, give attendance to reading, to exhortation, to doctrine." 1 Tim 4:13

One major indispensable part of living is feeding. It's a major part of every living thing. There is absolutely no way we can stay alive without feeding on a daily basis. Even if you don't like eating, you'll still do it daily no matter how small. Just as we physically depend on food for strength, growth and sustainability so we need the word of God to remain spiritually strong and relevant. Once the place of the word is missing in our lives spiritual weakness will begin to set in gradually. It usually does not happen at once; this is why it may not be noticed on time.

I want to spend some days to help you to understand how to get the best out of the word of God and be robustly fed by the word.

There must be a daily reading and studying of the word of God. This is where the journey begins from. One of the things God's word does is to build us up and prepare us for the day of challenge. The day of challenge usually will not give us a notice. Its therefore important to stay prepared and equipped to face whatever comes our way in life. Its important we pick a portion of scriptures that we'll read for a period. Its usually not right to read haphazardly.

As we sit down daily to read and study the word of God it may not look as if anything serious is taking place. But we must realise that the word of God is a spiritual material that keeps working as we apply our hearts to it. When a seed is sown in the ground it may not necessarily grow and produce fruits the same day. But as long as the seed remains in the soil it will eventually grow out and go through several stages of growth and a full harvest for the farmer. "Let them not depart from thine eyes; keep them in the midst of your heart." Prov 4:21

PRAYER:

Lord I receive the grace and the discipline to stay with your word on a daily basis.

LEARN MORE: Prov 4:20-22, 1 Peter 2:2

PRAYER REQUEST: Lord we receive fresh daily grace over Inspiration to change lives daily. John 1:16

CONSULTING
THE AUTHOR

———— ∞∞∞ ————

Text: "All scripture is given by Inspiration of God..." 2Tim 3:16

Every book we have ever read is an expression of the thoughts and the intentions of an author. It will be absolutely impossible to understand a book without seeing it from the perspective of the author. If we look casually at the word of God it may seems that men authored it; but its clear from the word of God that men were only prompted or moved by someone to write. The words these men wrote emanated from someone. Men like Moses, Peter, Paul and the rest were mere pencils in the hand of the creator.

Please read this scripture carefully *"For the prophecy came not in old time by the will of man: but holy men of God spake as they were moved by the Holy Ghost." 2 Peter 1:21.* Its therefore clear that the Holy Spirit is the author of the word of God. If we are going to get the best out of God's word, we must consciously consult the author. Only him knows the mind of God and what God wants to communicate to us per time.

Jesus clearly told the disciples *"I have yet many things to say unto you, but ye cannot bear them now. Howbeit when he, the Spirit of truth, is come, he will guide you into all truth..." John 16:12-13.*

This makes it absolutely necessary to consult the author. He's our guide and our teacher. He wants to be actively involved as we go through the word. He wants to help us see what God is saying per time. The scripture also talks about the *"…Words which the Holy Ghost teacheth…" 1 Cor 2:13.* God also declared *"…I will pour out my Spirit unto you, I will make my words known unto you." Proverbs 1:23b.*

Each time you read your Bible or read a scripture related material like this one ask the Holy Spirit to teach you. By the infilling of the Spirit we are living temples of the Holy Ghost; we must therefore be conscious of his presence and engage him.

PRAYER:

Holy Spirit you are my guide and my teacher. I open my heart to receive from you today.

LEARN MORE: John 14:26, 1 Cor 2:9-13

PRAYER REQUEST: Lord we declare that there will be direction in the hearts of everyone reading Inspiration today. Ecc 10:10

OPENNESS OF HEART

⸺◦◦◦⸺

Text: "Lydia…Whose heart the Lord opened, that she attended unto the things which were spoken of Paul." Acts 16:14

The word of God is designed to accomplish certain things in our lives. There should be a change and transformations taking place as we interact with the word of God. The extent to which this will take place will depend on the extent to which our hearts are open to receive God's word and to make changes in our lives.

The word of God will challenge our thoughts and change set patterns in our lives. Most times what God's word will ask us to do will not be popular and widely accepted. The word of God will teach, reproof, correct and direct. If our hearts are not open it won't happen.

Openness of heart is expressed in the following ways:

1. You have a teachable spirit.* You are always eager to learn and always open to receive more of what God has in store.

2. You are not rigid on opinions; you are flexible with God.*

3. You don't mind asking questions from people that may even be younger or less placed than you in life.*

4. You don't try in any way to make excuses for anything once the word of God convicts you of it.*

5. The word of God holds the final authority in your life.*

6. You are ready to submit to whatever it says.* Every form of argument is stopped.

If we are not open to God's word its effects will be minimal or completely absent in our lives. God and his word are one and the extent to which we open our hearts to the word is a direct indication of how open we are to God. God is on the look out for such people whose hearts are completely yielded to him.

PRAYER:

Lord I declare that my heart is continually opened to receive your word and to be changed by it.

LEARN MORE: James 1:21

PRAYER REQUEST: Lord we declare that new doors of favour, increase and promotion are opening for everyone reading Inspiration. Isa 43:19

HELPED BY THE SPIRIT

⸺⸺∞⸺⸺

Text: "And Pharoah said unto his servants, Can we find such a one as this is, a man in whom the Spirit of God is?" Gen 41:38

There are several people in scriptures that had extraordinary lives. They all went through several challenges in life that naturally would have destroyed them but they came out of it stronger and victorious. What was that major factor that made the difference in their lives? What was it that they had that others did not have? These are the questions we want to answer in this article today.

Joseph had one of the most difficult task to handle. He needed to interpret the dream of the king and also provide the answer. According to Pharaoh there is none that can interpret it. All the magicians and wise men of the land had tried to no avail. At the end of the day Joseph was able to interpret it and also provide the solution. Then Pharaoh gave his response *"...Can we find such a one as this is, a man in whom the Spirit of God is?" (Gen 41:38).* The interpretation was purely done by the Spirit of God. This placed Joseph on the throne in a foreign land. Someone is reading this; this is your time of supernatural enthronement. The Spirit of God in the next seven weeks will take you to a place you never thought you could get to in seven years. It will be so dramatic that celebration will never cease in your life. Joseph was helped by the Spirit.

The Philistines were out to completely destroy Samson. Several strategies were devised to get him destroyed. In each of the cases he came out victorious. It was not because he was a giant; there is no reference in scriptures that said he was a giant. He was just an ordinary person like every other person. It was the anointing of the Spirit on his life that helped him. According to him if he's shaven and the anointing of the Spirit is lifted he will become like an ordinary man. We can go on and on to give several examples of great exploits in scriptures. It was all because this people were helped by the Spirit of God.

PRAYER:

Lord I open my heart and my life to the help of your Spirit in every area of my life.

LEARN MORE: Judges 14:5-6; 16:8-9, Acts 26:22

PRAYER REQUEST: Lord we declare that everyone reading Inspiration will take root downward and bear fruits upwards. Isa 37:31

IT'S NOT LATE YET

Text: "Then said Martha unto Jesus, Lord, if thou hadst been here, my brother had not died." John 11:21

Jesus was told that Lazarus was sick and for some reason he did not get there until the man had died. When he eventually arrived there the sister spoke to him "If you had come earlier my brother would not have died." (Paraphrase). She was more or less saying Jesus you came too late. Jesus explained to them that he will rise again. The sister assumed that Jesus was referring to the resurrection of the last day.

The response of Jesus to all this was completely different from human thinking. He arrived late based on time; but he was not late in divine calculation. He explained to them "I am the resurrection and the life..." The number of days the man had died was not a barrier to him. It was humanly impossible based on the analysis of the Sisters but as far as Jesus was concerned "This is sickness is not unto death..." He had spoken that word earlier and it must come to pass.

As far as God is concerned nothing is too late in our lives. Age may be saying it's over with us; but God is saying it's not over yet. Saying it's too late is more or less writing off the possibility of anything good coming out of that situation? God does not write anything off in our lives. He promised to give us a new beginning. With God there can be a new beginning for anything and anyone.

There is someone reading this today the past events of your life is telling you that nothing good can come out of your life again; but it's a lie of the devil. It's not late for you yet; if you'll genuinely yield your life to God today he will give you a brand new beginning. Situations are turning around in your favour from today.

PRAYER:

Father thank you because it's not too late for me yet. There is a new beginning taking place in my life.

LEARN MORE: Isa 43:19

PRAYER REQUEST: Lord we ask that your manifest presence will go with your people today. Heb 13:5-6

LEAVING ALL BEHIND

Text: "By faith Abraham when he was called to go out into a place which he should after receive for an inheritance, obeyed; and he went out, not knowing whither he went." Heb 11:8

Faith for so many of us is just a means of getting a new car, getting the biggest car in town, getting someone to marry etc. If you look closely at the life of the patriarchs of faith you will see that faith is far bigger than that. Faith is more of the ability to follow God without any reservation. Another word for faith is abandoning your life to God and his word.

Abraham was an old man. He had lived with his kindred for decades; now God was asking him to leave the familiar environment and the convenience of his community. He was going to leave all this behind for a journey to a place he was not even sure of. This is an example of leaving all behind to reach for the best that God has to offer. He must have believed that God cannot mismanage his life. He must have realised that whatever God has in store ahead was far bigger and better than all he has seen so far in life.

At certain times in our lives we may have to leave certain things behind to reach for God's ultimate plan for our lives. This is the greatest walk of faith any of us could engage in. This is a journey that takes us from the known to the unknown. The best of God for our lives are actually in places that we presently may consider as the unknown. We must therefore be ready for such moments where God will require that we leave certain things behind to move by faith into his original intents for our lives from the foundation of the earth. If your concept about God is all about getting shoes, cloths and make ups from him your walk with God will be childish and very shallow. We need to move to higher realms of faith where we wait to see the direction of the Spirit and we move there by faith. The wife of Lot became a pillar of salt because she could not leave all behind; she was so used to life is Sodom. Let go today!

PRAYER:

In the name of Jesus I leave behind everything that is no longer in agreement with God's plans and purpose for me.

LEARN MORE: Gen 12:1-7

PRAYER REQUEST: We break every chain that may be holding anyone reading Inspiration down, we release them into purpose. Jeremiah 11:29

GROWING IN LOVE

Text: "And the Lord make you to increase and abound in love one toward another, and toward all men, even as we do toward you." 1 Thess 3:12

The greatest expression of God at work in a man is the rate at which the love of God is expressed through such a man. Christianity is actually the expression of the divine nature through a mortal man. This is an experience that should keep growing and expanding in the life of a believer.

The phrase "Increase and abound" in our anchor scripture simply talks about "growth." Every divine virtue at work in a believer has the capacity to grow. The more this virtue grows in us the more the beauty of our lives is expressed all around us.

As we grow in love the more our lives becomes a force of attraction. We can literally begin to draw others to God by the fragrance of our lives. Let me give you a couple of signs that you are growing in love:

I. There will be a passion in you to reach out to people around you to be a positive influence on their lives. There will always be a desire in you to add value to other people.

II. There will be the ability to let go easily and freely over every offence.

III. You have a heart of compassion for the plight of people around you. If you are so preoccupied by what you are going through and hardly notice others it's a sign of selfishness.

IV. You have come to place value on people and to see God in them in everything. This will be revealed in how you talk to them and how you respond to them.

The opposite of love is actually selfishness. It will be difficult to influence anyone positively this way.

PRAYER:

Lord I declare that your kind of love is finding expression in my life. My life has become an oasis of love.

LEARN MORE: 1 Cor 13:1-8

PRAYER REQUEST: In the name of Jesus we ask that everyone reading Inspiration will stand perfect and complete in all the will of God.

GROWING IN GRACE

---∞∞∞---

Text: "But grow in grace, and in the knowledge of our Lord and savior Jesus Christ. To him be glory both now and for ever. Amen." 2 Peter 3:18

Grace in our context today is the divine enablement that works in a man to do the unusual and go beyond the ordinary. Grace is divinity at work in humanity thereby making the man divine in accomplishment. We all need this dimension of the grace of God to find expression in our lives.

Grace is elastic. It can grow to whatever degree we desire it. We can never get to a point in our lives where we've had enough of the grace of God. The more you have the more you will need. As we grow in grace so also the depth of our results in life is enhanced. Where we are today and what we have seen so far in life is a function of the level of grace we have enjoyed. There should be a craving in your life to grow in grace and function at an higher level of life.

Grace grows in our lives as the rate of our dependency on God grows. This requires a heart of humility; a heart that submits to God in everything. The more a man resists God the more a man deprives himself of the grace of God. Grace is a function of dependency on God. When you are embarking on an assignment let it be evident that you are heavily depending on God. Express it verbally; let everyone around you know that you are depending on God. Let it never be said that you did anything on your own. With such dependence we'll always go to God in prayer.

We also grow in grace as we ensure that every level of grace that we have is maximally utilised. If you waste one level of grace you cannot grow beyond that level. Why will God add more to you if you have not utilised the previous; it will obviously be wasted too. Get busy at your current level of grace and watch yourself grow.

PRAYER:

Lord I need more of your grace over my life in everything I do. I depend solely upon you in everything and for everything.

LEARN MORE: Prov 3:5-6, Heb 4:16

PRAYER REQUEST: Lord we declare that everyone reading Inspiration will be established and settled in Divine purpose. 1 Peter 5:10

GROWING IN STRENGTH

⸺◦∞∞◦⸺

Text: "They go from strength to strength, everyone of them in Zion appeareth before God." Psalm 84:7

The phrase "…Strength to strength…" is an expression of growth. We are not just talking of physical strength but rather spiritual strength. Spiritual strength is a function of our inner man. Men are controlled by the state of their spirit and not just what goes on in the environment. The happening in the environment takes control of a man when the spirit man is in a weak state.

Please read this scripture with me "The spirit of a man will sustain his infirmity, but a wounded spirit who can bear?" (Prov 18:14). NIV says "A man's spirit sustains him in sickness, but a crushed spirit who can bear." The extent to which this will happen in our lives will depend on the level of spiritual strength in our spirit.

The more we grow in strength spiritually the more we can handle external challenges that come our way. According to the details available in scripture King Saul was a very tall man. He was shoulder high than every other person. Obviously he had some levels of physical strength. According to scriptural details too he was fully armed with a sword and a shield to fight in a battle. Despite all these he could not face Goliath. David was completely far away from what King Saul had. The difference between both of them was simply spiritual strength. King Saul was big physically but small spiritually. David was small physically but big spiritually.

From our anchor scripture "Zion" is not just a building but a place of spiritual engagement. The more we engage ourselves productively spiritually the more we grow in spiritual strength. This has to become a major prayer point for us. Ephesians 3:16 says "That he would grant you, according to the riches of his glory, to be strengthened with might by his Spirit in the inner man." We are strengthened by the spirit.

PRAYER:

In the name of Jesus I am strengthened by God's Spirit in my spirit. I'm going from strength to strength.

LEARN MORE: Eph 3:16, 2 Cor 4:16

PRAYER REQUEST: Lord quicken your people afresh by your Spirit to do your will. John 6:63

GROWING IN SERVICE

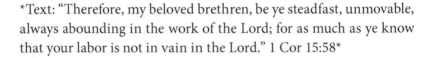

Text: "Therefore, my beloved brethren, be ye steadfast, unmovable, always abounding in the work of the Lord; for as much as ye know that your labor is not in vain in the Lord." 1 Cor 15:58

Salvation is a free gift without paying any price on our part. It was completed, sealed and delivered to us wholesale. The main fact that salvation is free does not mean that after we are saved we should sit down and do nothing. There is a response required on our part as a way of appreciation for all that God had wrought through Christ in our lives.

The word "abound" in our opening scripture means to keep increasing in something. God's expectation is that we do the work of the Lord. This simply means active involvement in kingdom service. This should be something that is done in an increasing measure.

Growing in service simply means growing in usefulness. Each one of us as believers is designed for the "master's use" (2 Tim 2:19). If a man is not useful to God he's really of no use in life because the only thing that holds real value is what is done for God.

We grow in usefulness as we look for more opportunities to be a blessing to people around us. Human need is inexhaustible. There will always be a need around us that needs someone to rise up to the occasion. I was doing quite well serving a local Church several years back. At a point I felt there was a need to find something for our church members to read on a daily basis. I started writing and printing on A4 papers to cover for a whole week. After a while I began to print in a book form. As we grow in grace just as we said a couple of days ago we'll realise that we'll also grow in usefulness. Growing in service means we are covering more grounds; touching more lives. Let this be your conviction "there is nothing done in vain." God is watching every seed of service in the kingdom. This is the greatest investment our lives.

PRAYER:

In the name of Jesus I'm increasing in usefulness. My life is making so much difference in the kingdom.

LEARN MORE: Ps 22:30, Rom 12:11

PRAYER REQUEST: Lord we declare that grace will be at work in everyone reading Inspiration not to miss there due seasons. Gal 6:9

[7/26/2019, 5:31 PM] +234 813 850 8568: Forwarded message:

Good morning, Peace be unto every one hearing my voice, this is God's message to every body most especially, "G.O" FOUNDERS OF THE CHURCH, God said book haram has joined forces with Fulani herdsmen, in Nigeria, they have strategized and gathered armnations and weapons and about to set for WAR, God said all men of God should stand up against the this war, most especially the PROPHETS, many have lost their positions, they are only seeking earthly NAME and POSITION, we don't stand for Nigeria, God said we should stand up now, and HE "GOD" is ready to stop the war and deliver NIGERIA from civil war, for this reason you are hearing me this morning, GOD said for good 3 weeks we should embrace service of praise in each Church, that is what God will use, we should call on God of DAVID and GOD of MOSES, God said in the same manner that HE delivered ISRAEL from Philistines and Egypt, HE is set to deliver NIGERIA, but if we don't do this, WAR is upon us, God said, all men of God if you don't do this, you will suddenly discover that enemy will burn down your families and your worshiping centers, and every body will bear the SIN thereby, therefore, God is set to deliver NIGERIA, by embracing this three weeks "3" service of praise by reading EXODUS 15 and CHRONICLES 16 vs 8 - 34, GOD said we should call forth ministering angels of songs upon NIGERIA, for a massive war supporting, while HE GOD will lay ambush against all NIGERIANS ENEMIES, GOD said send this message to all Churches as quickly as you received it, I beg you in the name of CHRIST and also in GOD'S name upon whom we shall give account, WOE BETIDES ME if I do not deliver this message, please help me send it all over NIGERIA, and we shall be free from war, and PEACE shall REIGN in NIGERIA, the WONDERS of God shall happen in our life as we send this message, PEACE be unto us in JESUS NAME.

GROWING IN PURITY

———— ∞∞∞ ————

Text: "Take away the dross from the silver and there shall come forth a vessel for the finer". Prov 25:4

The value of precious stones like gold increases with the degree of purity. The purer it becomes the more valuable it becomes. The material goes through a refining process that ensures that the impurities are removed to increase its value. This is also true of a believer. The worth and usefulness of a metal depends so much on its purity. This is why the metal has to go through the process of purification to make it valuable and use able. This is a natural process that applies to our lives as believers.

God is on the lookout for men and women that he can use and make a showpiece on the earth. God can use anything but then the degree to which he will use us depends on the level of our purity. Whatever defiles you disqualifies you for higher levels of usefulness.

When the "dross" in our lives is taking away we become extremely useful in the hands of God.

God goes an extra mile to pour his grace into our lives as we make ourselves available for him.

God actually works through men to do whatever he wants to do on the earth. You don't need a title to be used of God; all you need is a pure heart and a right spirit.

Dross could mean a wrong mindset, a sinful habit or even things that are legitimate that has become a hindrance to God's access into our lives. It could be a human relationship that has taken the place of God in our lives. The "dross" is removed in our lives as we subject our hearts to the word of God. The Spirit of God takes hold of the word to purify our hearts. We are purified by the word of God because the word itself has been tested and purified seven times in fire. As we grow in purity so also we begin to grow in wisdom and power.

PRAYER:

Lord purify my hearts, purify my entire being and work in me by your Spirit to be a vessel unto honour.

LEARN MORE: 2 Tim 2:19-21, John 17:17

PRAYER REQUEST: Lord sanctify your people afresh this week by your word through Inspiration. John 17:17

GROWING INTO MATURITY

———— ⦵⦵⦵ ————

Text: "When I was a child, I spake as a child, I understood as a child, I thought as a child: but when I became a man, I put away childish things." 1 Cor 13:11

Maturity is not so much a function of age; it's more a function of our thought process. Maturity is often revealed in our words. When you hear an individual talking one can conclude whether this is an adult or a child. So many are adults in age but childish in their way of thinking and talking.

One of the greatest privileges of life is the privilege of growth. It does not really matter what level of maturity we are right now we can grow to higher levels of maturity. The more matured we become the more responsible we become and the more dependable we become. These two traits are so important to human existence. Great businesses are built by responsible and dependable people. A great marriage needs responsible and dependable people. A country needs responsible and dependable leaders. Each one of us must have a resolve to be responsible and dependable.

As believers we become matured in proportion to which the word of God takes over our thought pattern. "...I spake as a child, I understood as a child, I thought as a child..." I want you to note that a child's way of talking, understanding and thinking is usually shallow. As the word of God takes over us, we begin to think, understand and talk like God. The way we see life becomes exactly like God. This is the highest definition of maturity. If someone offends you for example the way you respond to it will reveal your level of maturity. The word of God gives all of us a common yardstick to determine the thought that is childish and that which is matured. If you allow the word of God to truly take over your life you'll become highly responsible and dependable.

CONFESSION:

As I read this material daily the word of God is growing in me and I am growing in maturity.

LEARN MORE: Acts 20:32, 1 Pet 2:2

PRAYER REQUEST: In the name of Jesus we bring into judgment whatever may be working against anyone reading Inspiration. Isa 54:14

POWER OF CONSCIENCE

Text: "And they which heard it, being convicted by their own conscience, went out one by one, beginning at the eldest, even unto the last...." John 8:9

Let's close this month with these thoughts. This group of men had caught a woman right in the act of adultery. Acting on the content of the law, they dragged the woman to Jesus to receive her judgment. Then Jesus went on to ask anyone who has never sinned before to be the first person to cast a stone at the woman. At the end of the day the men left one after the other.

One good thing about these men was that they still had a functioning conscience. These men were convicted by their conscience. Their conscience helped them to appreciate their own state. It was not as if someone came to expose their problem to them. It was their conscience that did it. The conscience is an inner guard, an inner police man that puts a check and a restriction on a man. To live above sin we need a conscience that is tender and sensitive. Constant exposure to sin could harden the conscience. This brings us to a point where we begin to look at certain things as normal even though God disapproves of them.

The scriptures describe a state in which the conscience is defiled. This is a terrible state that any of us cannot afford to get to. The conscience begins to approve and endorse wrong thing. A conscience seared with hot iron is one that does not even listen again. In this state people prefer to say and hear lies rather than the truth (Titus 1:15, 1 Tim 4:2).

A pure conscience will put a check and a restriction on our lives. With this we speak truth to ourselves. I'm sure that it was the pure conscience of Joseph that helped him to run away from his master's wife even though nobody was with them.

PRAYER:

Lord help me by your Spirit to have a conscience that is void of offence. That it may approve things that are pure.

LEARN MORE: Acts 24:16, Heb 9:14

*PRAYER REQUEST: Lord we declare that every copy of Inspiration that will get to the prisoners will be a tool to transform lives. 2

PRAYING FOR PRISONERS:

Please join me daily!

In the name of Jesus we decree that your word through Inspiration will grow and prevail in prison houses across the nations of the earth. Acts 19:20

The Lord reward you!

Inspiring Men!

"Temptation gains its power in secrecy. If sin is not exposed and repented of on time it will gain root and make us weaker. David was a man after God's heart because he was quick to repent." BE A MAN!

*Read through Proverbs

Read one chapter daily that correspond to the date of the day. Then post one verse on your status each day!

FORGOTTEN IN PRISON

Text: "Yet did not the chief butler remember Joseph; but forget him." Gen 40:23

Joseph successfully helped the butler to interpret his dream. The dream literally came to pass. The butler was fully restored back to his position. He was now in a position to reciprocate back to Joseph. But somehow, he forgot. Joseph was again left in prison for about two (2) years. It seems the prison term had no end.

God had to supernaturally orchestrate how he will come out. Many had been forgotten by relatives, friends and colleagues. Many family members have forgotten their loved ones in prison. They seem not to care anymore. It was the same experience for Joseph. His family did not even know he was in prison. The person he helped also forgot him.

It's important for us to note that there is a God who does not forget us. He promised never to leave us nor forsake us. He promised to be with us till the end of the age. Men may forget but God does not. Don't ever use what men did as definition for who God is in your life.

All over scripture we have the promise and the assurance of a God who never forgets us. Isaiah 49:15 God declared *"Never! Can a mother forget her nursing child? Can she feel no love for the child she has borne? But even if that were possible, I would not forget you! (NIT) * With this depth of divine assurance David declared *"Even if my father and mother abandon me, the Lord will hold me close. Psalm 27:10 (NLT)."* We have a divine assurance that we are always on God's mind. We are engraved on the palms of his hands. In the fullness of time a book of remembrance will be opened concerning us. God is behind the scene of a life that holds on to him. His counsels will come to pass in your life at the due time. It was as if Joseph was forgotten but the God who never forgets opened the book of remembrance concerning him. He found himself in the palace where no one never thought he will reach.

CONFESSION:

I declare that I am never forgotten. I'm always on God's mind.

LEARN MORE: Hebrew 13:5-6

PRAYER REQUEST: In the name of Jesus we decree that there is a daily transformation taking place in the lives of everyone reading Inspiration. 2 Cor 3:18

Inspiring Men!

"One thing is sure, we cannot be full of ourselves and be full of God at the same time. We need the fullness of God in our lives to amount to anything significant." BE A MAN!

PREPARED IN PRISON

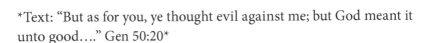

Text: "But as for you, ye thought evil against me; but God meant it unto good…." Gen 50:20

The man who wins the boxing championship did not necessarily begin in the ring. He must have begun somewhere that nobody knew him. He must have began hidden from the eyes of men. He must have begun in a place that attracted no remuneration. The manifestations in the ring were prepared in the dark and hidden places. This is exactly how life is designed to play out for people that will end up great in life.

God will use dark and hidden places to prepare people for where he had prepared for them in life. For Joseph it was the house of Potiphar and the prison that God used to prepare him for the palace.

His administrative ability found greater expression in the prison. He was there for over two (2) years and there he was able to know how to manage certain resources committed to his hands. It was the same thing he did in the house of Potiphar. I'm sure you can still recollect that he was so loved by his father. He was the son of his old age. He had so many elder ones and no one would have exposed him to responsibilities required for the throne. The "prison" experience was a preparation experience for him.

Secondly, he was cheerful enough to recognise the sad countenance of the Baker and the Butler. He eventually helped in the interpretation of their dreams. This actually prepared him for the future. At the time he was interpreting for the servants he never knew that the same dimension of opportunity is what will bring him out of prison and establish the purpose of God that he saw at the age of seventeen. By the time the opportunity came he was prepared for it.

Nothing in life is a waste. Every experience you go through will prepare you for something greater than where you are. Stay open and connected to God; there is purpose in your pain.

PRAYER:

Thank you, Lord, for every experience life has ever brought my way. Thank you for the "throne" ahead.

LEARN MORE: James 1:2-4

PRAYER REQUEST: Lord we declare that your word takes preeminence in the lives of everyone reading Inspiration. Job 23:12

Inspiring Men!

"The best demonstration of love to children is not necessarily the toys or the chocolates but the quality time spent with them and the attention given to them. They will outgrow the toys but wont outgrow the affection of a father." BE A MAN!

DISCOVERY IN PRISON 1

Text: "And Joseph answered and said, this is the interpretation thereof..." Genesis 40:18

There is no restriction to where God can reveal himself and his plans for our lives. The discovery of God's purpose and plan for our lives mostly will take place in unexpected places and circumstances. This is why our spiritual antenna and receptivity to God must be continually open. Joseph found himself in a hopeless situation. Right in the prison the power of God was still at work in him.

His family actually thought he was dead. Humanly speaking there was no way out for him. In the midst of all these the gift of God was still finding expression in Joseph. Like we said before he did not allow his environment to condition him. He was in prison but the prison was not in him. What happen to us is not as important as what happen in us. Even in the worst scenario of life we can locate a way out as long as we don't allow it to condition our mindset. Joseph was still productive in the worst condition of life. There was no record of ever interpreting dreams for anyone until he got to the prison. It was the same dream that took him out of prison into the palace. What if he had not discovered it? The greatest breakthroughs of our lives are simply a discovery away.

With the right disposition to adversity the best of our lives can come out of it. The worst conditions of life can work out to our greatest advantage. Whatever you may be going through right now keep yourself open and connected to God. It was not God that took Joseph to the prison, but God used it for his glory. Whatever is designed to harm you will be used for the glory of God. JOSEPH'S RELEVANCE BECAME OBVIOUS IN THE PRISON. WHERE YOU ARE NOW MAY NOT BE GOOD BUT IT CAN BE THE STARTING POINT OF A GREAT FUTURE.

CONFESSION:

I'm not disadvantaged in life. The hand of God is working out the details of my life. I'm coming out better.

LEARN MORE: Rom 8:28-39

PRAYER REQUEST: Lord we ask for a fresh outpouring of your Spirit over the daily reading of Inspiration. Joel 2:28

Inspiring Men!

"The highest level of ignorance is when you don't know and you don't know that you don't know. Crave for more knowledge; it will make you a better man." BE A MAN!

PASTOR DAVID

DISCOVERY IN PRISON 2

———∞∞∞———

Text: "And Joseph answered and said, this is the interpretation thereof..." Genesis 40:18

There is a divine package in our recreated human spirit that is designed to make room for us in life. We may not have a rich pedigree or powerful connections that can make away for us but the ability of God in our spirit can make a room for us. Prov 18:16 says "A man's gift makes room for him..." NKJV. Myles Munroe said "It is interesting to note that the Bible did not say that a man's education makes room for him, but that his gift does" He also said "When you exercise your gift, not only will the world make room for you, but it will pay you for it."

Joseph began the interpretation of dreams in the prison.
Considering where he was, he would have been sad and question God.
What happen to us is not as important as what happen in us.
Even in the worst scenarios of life we can locate a way out as long as we don't allow it to condition our mindset.

I. The purpose of God can be revealed in the midst of a terrible Job.

II. A disappointment in life can be the birth place of a great destiny.

III. A mess can become a message.

Joseph discovered his individuality in the prison! *Individuality is the divine signature coded in every human spirit.*

Individuality is doing what is unique to you in your God given unique way. Individuality is the key to standing out in life. If you don't *discover,* *develop* and *deploy* your individuality you may get lost in the sea of humanity. By the gift of God expressed in our lives we can become so *valuable* and *productive* that doors will open for us. Let's close by saying that the presence of the Holy Spirit is the key to this discovery.

PRAYER:

The Spirit of God is working in me to bring me into divine discoveries of divine purpose and intent.

LEARN MORE: Gen 41:38, 1 Corinth 2:9-1

PRAYER REQUEST: Lord we rebuke every hindrance to the continuous spread of God's word through Inspiration.

PASTOR DAVID *Inspiring Men!*

"Excuses are the tools that men with no purpose in view use in building for themselves great monument of nothing. Stop the excuses it produces mental lameness." BE A MAN!

PRISON DOORS ARE OPEN

〰️

Text: "The Spirit of the Lord God is upon me, because the Lord hath anointed me to preach good tidings unto the meek; he hath sent me to bind up the broken-heated…and the opening of the prison to them that are bound." Isa 61:1

The prison mentioned here could be a physical prison but majorly it's a figurative statement. Its a word that describes a state of life. This scripture prophetically declares the primary mission of the messiah on earth. Jesus himself confirmed this mission in Luke chapter four verse eighteen. He came among others to open the prison to them that are bound.

The "prison" is a place of incarceration. It's a place where you are restricted and confined. It's a state of life where you realist you can't do what you are ordained to do. So many are bound by their past and seems never to get away from it. Some are bound by diverse kind of abuse in their past. Unfulfilled expectations have kept many bound in hopelessness. Many had given up on life.

The good news is that included in the package of the gospel is the opening of the prison to them that are bound. The sacrifice of Christ on the cross included the opening of the prison doors. There is absolutely nothing that has the right to hold us down any more. Once a man receives Christ, he receives instant liberty from all that must have held him down. Primarily we have been set free from the prison house of sin. The hold of sin has been broken over our lives. We are new creations today; old things are passed away in our lives and all things have become new.

Today God expects us to take a stand of faith in the reality of all what Christ has done for us. We must refuse every form of bondage today. The prison doors are open. You are free!

PRAYER:

Lord I declare that I am free. The prison doors are open. Nothing in the past, present or future can hold me down anymore.

LEARN MORE: Gal 5:1

PRAYER REQUEST: Lord we ask for divine appearances via your word in Inspiration to your people.

wa.me/+23470685053

THE NEED OF SALVATION 1

———— ⨯⨯⨯ ————

Text: "…Now is the accepted time; behold, now is the day of salvation." Isa 32:15

There were two (2) prominent men that came to Jesus at different times. Both of them were highly placed people. Both of them must have realized the emptiness of their soul. Their prominence and status in the society could not fill the void in their souls.

Nicodemus was a highly religious Jewish leader and respected by his people. It was obvious that his religion was not enough to save him so he came to Jesus secretly in the night. Jesus took his time to explain to him that he needed to be born again. His religious mindset could not comprehend what Jesus was saying (John 3:1-9). It's important for us to realize that religion does not save a man. That you were born inside a church and had been there all your life is not a guarantee that you are saved. Salvation is a definite encounter with Jesus with a spiritual transformation.

The second man was the rich ruler. He came to Jesus and asked the question "…Good master, what good thing shall I do, that I may have eternal life? (Matthew 19:16)." This obviously meant that he did not have eternal life yet. If eternal life was to be purchased with money, he would have acquired it with his money. When it comes to salvation our money is useless. The human soul is worth more than the whole world put together. This man also did not realize that there is no number of good things that gets a man saved. The word of God declared "Not by works of righteousness which we have done, but according to his mercy he saved us, by the washing of regeneration, and renewing of the Holy Spirit (Titus 3:5)."

If you are reading this today, I want to ask you to check the state of your soul. Are you truly saved or playing religion? Your years in Church does not equal salvation. We'll conclude this tomorrow.

CONFESSION:

I need you Jesus. I need you as my Lord and savior. I acknowledge my sin. Jesus take over my heart today.

LEARN MORE: John 3:1-6, Rom 10:1-12

PRAYER REQUEST: We ask for fresh help of the Holy Spirit on fresh impact of God's word through Inspiration. Joel 2:28

PAGE 60

THE NEED OF SALVATION 2

———— ∞∞∞ ————

Text: "…Now is the accepted time; behold, now is the day of salvation." 2 Cor 6:2

Let's continue our lesson today from where we left off yesterday. We saw how Nicodemus and the rich ruler came to Jesus seeking to know how to be saved.

The good thing is that these two men came to Jesus. They were humble enough to admit their need of eternal life. They must have also realized that there is no other name under heaven by which men might be saved apart from the name of Jesus (Acts 4:12). Whosoever shall call on the name of Jesus shall be saved. (Rom 10:13). This is the day of salvation. The price has been fully paid. Jesus went to the cross and shed his blood for the remission of our sins. He took upon himself the nature of a man and died in our place. He took our sin and offered us the gift of his righteousness. When a man is not saved, he has settled for an eternal condemnation. Eternity is too long to lose our soul. (John 3:18, 2 Cor 5:21). The beauty about all this is that there is no sinner that is beyond redemption; no sin that the blood of Jesus cannot cleanse.

The scripture declared "That if thou shalt confess with thy mouth the Lord Jesus, and shall believe in thine heart that God hath raised him from the dead, thou shalt be saved. For with the heart man believe unto righteousness; and with the mouth confession is made unto salvation (Romans 10:9-10). This is the process of receiving salvation. Someone reading may need to do this today!

You can be saved even right now wherever you are. God is knocking at the door of your heart if you will open your heart to him. Pray with me and say loud "Jesus I confess you as my Lord and savior, I confess you died and resurrected for me. From today I'm born again. I'm saved." NOW YOU ARE SAVED!

PRAYER:

Lord I declare that I'm a child of God. I declare that I'm saved, washed and sanctified by the blood of Jesus.

LEARN MORE: 1 Corinth 6:9-11, 2 Corinth 5:17

PRAYER REQUEST: Lord we ask that everyone reading this devotional who are not yet saved will come under the convictions of the Holy Sprit.

Printed in the United States
By Bookmasters